Maybe It IS All in Your Head . . . and You Are NOT Crazy!

Russel Roby, J.D., M.D.

with Ric Keaster

Maybe It IS All in Your Head . . .
and You Are NOT Crazy!

Library of Congress Control Number: 2008907436
ISBN 978-0-9820646-0-3

First Edition

Printed in Canada

Published by
R&K Publishing
Austin, TX

Produced by
PPC Books
Redington Shores, FL

Table of Contents

Chapter 1

Good News and Bad News

➢ BAD NEWS

Are you one of the millions of people in the United States who physically suffers on a daily basis? Have you been to your doctor or, even more likely, a series of doctors who have run test after test on you, only to conclude there is nothing really wrong with you? The medical facts force the doctor to conclude that your pain or suffering is *all in your head.* Many, many people experience this every day from trusted physicians of every specialty. Or maybe you have been told you have a terrible disease that is almost always fatal. "There are no known causes, no effective treatment, and it might be related to the immune system." The most common of these are multiple sclerosis (MS), polymyositis, and idiopathic pulmonary fibrosis (IPF). I have successfully treated these disorders along with the less fatal but terribly debilitating condition known as interstitial cystitis, or IC.

➢ MAYBE YOUR DOCTOR IS WRONG

Let's start with the bad news disorders. Fortunately, doctors are often wrong. If you are having severe breathing problems and do not respond to medications like prednisone and albuterol, you might find yourself with increasing weakness and shortness of breath. As you get weaker and weaker, you may even be put on oxygen just so you can remain reasonably comfortable. This is usually the case with IPF. Then the doctor looks for other signs to help diagnose the problem. Things like x-ray or lung scans that might show lung changes that are seen in cases of IPF.

I have seen a few cases like this and the patient was told there was nothing more that could be done. The patient and the family were advised to prepare for a steady decline that could only result in death. In one recent case, the patient was told she had "less than a year to live." I knew the family so I invited the patient by to see if our sublingual progesterone drops might offer some relief of the shortness of breath. That is one of the things they do best (see "Progesterone as a Bronchodilator" in Revista Cientifica, 2007). In about ten minutes, the drops raised the patient's oxygen levels from 78% to 92%, on room air. This is impossible if you have IPF. So, what do we conclude? She didn't have IPF. She has progesterone–mediated inflammation. And we can treat that quite effectively. In minutes she was breathing much more easily and . . . she realized she wasn't going to die . . . at least not from the "IPF."

We have run into the same thing with severe cases of polymyositis and MS, where the patients were told they only had a short time to live. The polymyositis patient was told he only had one quarter of his lung capacity left. Yet in a matter of minutes, his oxygen went up from 80% to 97% which was almost three quarters of his lung capacity! He was reacting allergically to the hormone progesterone and that reaction was making his chest so rigid he could not move air. The drops blocked that reaction and in minutes, he was breathing deeply and speaking in normal tones with full breaths. What did we discover? He never had polymyositis. If he had, there would be no way to open his lungs up like that. What did he have? Progesterone–mediated inflammation.

One of our subjects in our paper mentioned above was diagnosed with end stage MS. She became part of our study because we enlisted subjects with "severe asthma." She was completely grey in pallor and could not speak in more than a whisper. She was so weak she had to be helped to a seat at the exam table and lay crumpled forward with her head on her arms. The first test indicated how little air she could move. Then we put drops of saline under her tongue as a "placebo control" and measured her breathing again. We saw the same numbers as the first test. Then we put the sublingual progesterone drops under her tongue and saw startling results. All her pulmonary function values went up. Dramatically up. Several went from a 250 to 400 improvement. She sat straight up and began to speak in a clear strong voice. Her skin became pink. What happened? She was severely allergic to the hormone progesterone and it kept her chest so rigid she could not breathe. When we blocked the progesterone-mediated inflammation with the sublingual drops, her symptoms were dramatically reduced in a matter of seconds.

These are just a few examples of how a diagnosis can be discarded, a death sentence reversed, if the symptoms used to reach the diagnosis can be reduced. Before we tell a patient there is nothing that can be done, shouldn't we at least try a few simple tests? Tests that are known to be effective, safe, and **cheap**? The test drops are made from Progesterone USP. That means we use 1/20th of a usual dose for the test and means we can get 1000 test doses from a stock vial of Progesterone USP available at most pharmacies for $40.00. So the tests cost about $0.50 each. Maybe it won't work in every case. But, what if it works half the time? Ten per cent of the time? If even a few lives are saved, it will surely be worthwhile trying.

This is an entire category of disorders we have been able to help. Whenever there is shortness of breath or severe pain that doesn't respond to standard treatment, shouldn't we explore all the possibilities before we condemn the patient? Isn't it amazing that the textbooks set out the information that there is "no effective treatment" for some conditions? And there never will be . . . unless medicine tries new things . . . unless patients demand new tests.

➢ GOOD NEWS – MAYBE IT IS ALL IN YOUR HEAD

The other, much larger group of patients I see are those who have been told there is "nothing wrong with you." They have been told their symptoms are "all in your head." There *has* to be something wrong. The human body does not, ordinarily, produce as much physical, mental, or emotional suffering as you are going through, unless something is wrong. In their defense I would point out that these doctors are doing precisely what they were trained to do . . . to detect and treat hundreds of *diseases*. They spent many years learning how to detect and treat these diseases. They are very good, probably the best in the world, at finding out what is wrong with people *if* they have one of the known *diseases*. They do an outstanding job of applying this knowledge to effectively treat these known disorders.

➢ YOUR TESTS ARE ALL "NORMAL"

However, what happens when the problem does not fit the definition of a *disease*? What if you have significant symptoms but no sign of a disease? What if the treatment of your symptoms doesn't work? What if the doctor can't find anything wrong with you? What if he (*see note at the end of the chapter) runs every test known to man and concludes you don't have any kind of disease? What if all your tests are "normal"? The doctor seems to take this attitude: "If I can't find it, you don't have it. In fact, in must be . . . all in your head." At this point, your doctor may suggest you go to a psychiatrist to deal with your problems. Some may offer a diagnosis that is non–specific, not a disease, but rather a *syndrome*. Syndromes are descriptions of a condition characterized by certain symptoms. Conditions like *fibromyalgia* or *irritable bowel syndrome* are described as syndromes when a certain number of symptoms are present. These aren't really diagnoses, but rather descriptions of what you related to the doctor. Irritable bowel syndrome means stomachache, for example. Arthritis (*arth* – joint, *itis* – inflammation) means "sore joint." That's what you told him. He is simply restating it and offering the description as his diagnosis.

In the absence of a disease as evidenced by "normal" lab studies and no physical signs the doctor can discover, and in the face of your continuing complaints of symptoms, some doctors may recommend an even more drastic diagnostic tool prior to consigning you to the local shrink, and that is . . . *exploratory surgery*. "We cannot find anything with blood tests. We may just have to go in there and take a look around." The problem with this approach is that the symptom may not have a specific location or pattern, being present some days and absent others. I don't recommend exploratory surgery before all other possibilities have been exhausted, including the drops we use.

In south Texas that is known as "sound shooting." Nimrod Yankees come down here for their first deer hunt. As they sit around a campfire late at night, armed to the teeth, they are primed for action. Then there is a pop or crack off in the brush and they all fire several shots in the direction of the sound. Many an innocent pickup truck has met its end in this fashion.

And here is a rule to live by: never ask a surgeon if he thinks you need surgery. If your regular doctor thinks you need surgery, then you might start trying to find one; but asking a surgeon about surgery is like asking a dairy farmer if you should drink milk. What do you *think* he is going to say? I want *three* physicians, who are not surgeons and who do not know one another, to all agree surgery is my only course of action. Then I will think about it some more and begin to look for the best surgeon I can find. By the way, Denton Cooley charged the same amount for a heart transplant at the Houston Medical Center as Dr. NoName in Austin, Texas. Informed consent should probably include the surgeon's success rate. Some, not surprisingly, are much better than others. Heart transplants have been going on at the rate of several per week in Houston since the 1960's. Just a few years ago, I saw a big spread in the Austin, Texas paper celebrating the first heart transplant at a local hospital. How would you like to be any city's *first* heart transplant?

Fortunately, most doctors stick with their first conclusion ("I don't think there is anything wrong with you") and usually don't refer these cases anywhere. So much for the bad news.

So, what's the good news? The good news is that the second part of their diagnosis may indeed be correct. Your pain and suffering truly ***is*** in your head; but not in the way that they are thinking. Their statement is intended to convince you that you are not really having this pain. You are either a "whacko" or a hypochondriac. Thus, they offer the suggestion that you might want to get some psychiatric help. Unfortunately, at this point many people begin to believe they *really might be* imagining the problem. Why else would they feel so bad? Why else when their doctor, whom they trust completely, is so certain there is nothing wrong with them? After all, he showed them the lab tests which clearly showed there was absolutely nothing wrong with them, at all.

➢ MAYBE IT IS ALL IN YOUR HEAD

Well, what if your symptoms are indeed in your head, but not in the way your doctor is suggesting? Your doctor has run every test there is to check for diseases and come up with nothing to explain your symptoms. But, maybe you don't have a *disease*, just the symptoms of some disease; or, as is often the case, of several diseases.

What if there can be other causes for symptoms that are not diseases? "Whoa!" exclaims the Doctor, "*There is nothing in* The Book *about that!*" Traditional medicine is not prepared to accept the possibility that something exists if it is not in their traditional textbooks, like conservatives are not prepared to accept liberalism. It seems that studies have demonstrated that we are biased in the way we gather information. We look for information that supports our prejudices. Thus, we end up in a sealed universe. Medical doctors believe in drugs and herbologists believe in herbs, to treat the same disorders. Most of us form our biases early and cling to them late. Traditional medicine thinks it knows *everything*. Thus, if it isn't in our traditional texts, studies, and literature (if it's not in The Book) . . . it doesn't exist. There is not even the *possibility* that it might exist.

➢ REDUCTIONISTS

Medicine seems bent on learning more and more about less and less. This is what Robert Laughlin (A Different Universe, 2005) refers to as *reductionist* thinking. Laughlin won the Nobel Prize in physics, and he points out that science wants to learn all about the smallest parts of a problem, thinking that information will allow them to solve the problem. He suggests that is a basic problem in physics and indeed, all of science, including medicine. These scientists define their own terms in their own areas of expertise and declare themselves *Masters of The Universe*, as they see it. Traditional medical doctors are reductionists who have boiled complex systems down to fit their beliefs. You either function normally or you have a disease which is a carefully defined abnormality which can be confirmed by tests and measurements. Nothing else exists for them. Either you have a disease . . . or you are normal. If you persist in describing symptoms that have no known cause, the reductionist doctor can only conclude that your symptoms are all in your head.

I think traditional medicine and their allies (health insurers, hospitals, and the pharmaceutical behemoths) are all deeply imbued with reductionist thinking. They have declared themselves masters of the science universe and they make up all the rules that govern it. They have staked their claim and they defend it vigorously. There is a huge amount of money and prestige involved in this high priesthood of reductionism we call Traditional Medicine. There is an entire industry revolving around health care and the treatment of disease. The medical establishment (doctors, nurses, and hospitals), the health insurance industry, and the pharmaceutical industry constitute a large segment of our entire economy and it is growing at the rate of about 18% per year.

I am going to propose something unthinkable. I am going to propose the possibility that as many as half of you aren't sick at all. I am going to propose that you may not even need a doctor. You may get rid of your symptoms using a safe, effective, cheap solution of a hormone placed under your tongue. Some "untreatable" diseases may be incorrectly diagnosed. If shortness of breath is the hallmark of IPF and we get rid of your shortness of breath, then clearly the diagnosis was incorrect.

What if that might actually be true? Now, picture this: what will the reaction of the health care industry be to news like that? What consternation would ensue if half of all health problems could be resolved by simply re-booting the brain (just as you might your computer) with some harmless drops? What will happen if all the interstitial cystitis patients (some scheduled for surgical removal of their bladders) insist on a test with sublingual progesterone drops . . . and their pain is dramatically reduced or eliminated? What do we think Medicine and Big Blue and Pharma are going to say about that? I think I might be in some trouble here. Well, let's take a look at it.

Laughlin (A Different Universe, 2005) uses what is supposed to be the world's most popular joke as an example of reductionist (medical) thinking. Sherlock Holmes and Dr. Watson are camping out:

> **Holmes**: Watson, look up at those stars in the sky! What do you deduce?
>
> **Watson**: Well, each of those pinpricks of light is a huge sun powered by the fires of hydrogen fusion. That fuzzy patch over there is the Andromeda galaxy. Powerful telescopes tell us that Andromeda is an island of billions and billions of stars. Even more powerful telescopes tell us that there are billions and billions of such galaxies stretching out to the edge of the universe. If even one in a million of those suns had planets, and even one in a million of these had an oxygen

> atmosphere, and even one in a million of these had life, and even one in a million of these had people and civilizations, then we would be certain of not being alone in the universe. *(Reductionist conclusion)*
>
> **Holmes**: No, Watson, you idiot! Someone stole our tent! *(Emergent conclusion)*

Medicine as we know it has been around for well over 100 years. Many of its most cherished principles go back over two centuries. This is an everlasting story: what was cherished in the past becomes even more sacred in the present. As soon as medicine began to believe in itself, it began to create the world of scientific thought in its own image. It could not do otherwise. Furthermore, it is natural for one's view of fact to be influenced by how one makes a living. This leads one more into mythology than fact. Now we have this enormously powerful mythology, medicine, and we find the doctors, bathed in the blood of this lamb, are going to enormous lengths to see the world of medicine and science as they think it should be, even when the evidence says they are mistaken. This leads us to what Laughlin refers to as the First Theorem of Science: It is impossible to convince a person of any true thing that will cost him money.

The best way to combat mythology in medicine is experimental application of previously unknown or untested new methods to deal with old problems. We don't have to invent new methods, we can discover them. Medicine considers this heresy. It is very protective of its field. Protection provides a stable and reliable means of dealing with known diseases, and at the same time it closes out the possibility of anyone ever discovering new solutions to the many unresolved issues in medicine. The industry of medicine busies itself with maintaining their tight grip on scientific method, on designing drugs to treat diseases and symptoms, and on inventing new health therapies. All this with no real understanding of the causes and regulatory mechanisms controlling the systems they deal with. Basically, they do not, in fact, know what they are doing. As Laughlin points out: "The fashion for tolerating ignorance of important scientific things is motivated not only by economics but also by politics. Scarcity of knowledge is considered good in some circles because it prevents wicked scientists from doing mischievous things."

➢ ANTITHEORIES

The science of medicine is simply a result of many decades of agreement by doctors who often do not know what they are doing. The fact that they have declared certain observations and principles to be truth itself, and then delivered it for political confirmation, simply enshrines and legitimizes its falsehoods. Most of our present–day medicine is ideological. That means it has no implications and cannot be tested. Remember, medicine thinks that over half of all symptoms are "all in your head." Medicine also is willing to say you are going to die and there is nothing that can be done for you. This is designed to stop innovative thinking rather than encourage it. Medicine claims it is a fact-based discipline, proving, over and over again, the truth of their methods with randomized, double-blinded, controlled studies. As such, no theories are helpful nor wanted. These are the antitheorists. The pig-headed response of the medical establishment to the innovative principles potentially present is an example of medicine's addiction to reductionist beliefs, happily abetted by the pharmaceutical industry, which greatly appreciates its role in the continued medication of symptoms.

<u>If you are going to die anyway, why not try something new?</u>

So, our question is, are we going to explore possible causes of problems and experiment with safe, innovative methods for dealing with them or just pass laws requiring everyone to remain ignorant of them?

I propose heresy! Anarchy! Drugless solutions to health problems! These solutions I propose are safe, quite effective, and cheap. That helps explain why I have had to defend myself from 20 complaints before the Texas Medical Board from 1985 to 2007. Not once have I been found to have injured any patient. I have repeatedly been found to have records that cannot be understood by traditional medical peers, and I have been compelled to tell you and every patient I see, that there is no scientific evidence to support any of the things I am going to tell you. I am further compelled to tell you and everyone I address that when I show you videos of my patients or when you read their stories, I have no scientifically accepted test that proves they are telling you the truth about their symptoms. I cannot prove they are really better. Galileo spent the last nine years of his life before he died in prison for his beliefs that the sun, not the earth, was the center of the universe. As Laughlin puts it, "The life of an anarchist is difficult and certainly not to be encouraged."

➢ EMERGENCE

Laughlin describes *emergence* as complex structure growing out of simple rules. He says, "Emergence means unpredictability, in the sense of small events (drops) causing great and qualitative changes in larger ones (symptoms)." The parenthetical inserts are mine. Emergence means the fundamental impossibility of control. If something as simple as a few drops of hormone gets rid of most of your symptoms, there can be no control. No proof. We will just have to take your word for it.

Which isn't always so. We have published our first study on "Progesterone as a Bronchodilator" (Roby R., Richardson P., Richardson R.H., & Shah, S., 2007) in Revista Cientifica, and in that study we demonstrated remarkable changes in actual pulmonary function tests. The progesterone drops caused a bronchodilator effect, as measured by spirometry, showing about a 75% improvement immediately after the progesterone drops were administered. In the most startling case, set out earlier, there was a 400% improvement in one area of pulmonary function.

Since we can't possibly expect any consideration from traditional doctors of possible causes of your problem other than *diseases*, let's ignore them for a bit and consider, for ourselves, some possible *causes* of symptoms that might not involve diseases.

➢ IMBALANCE

Your symptoms may be caused by an *imbalance*. Traditional doctors are not equipped to diagnose or treat you for possible a non–disease like an *imbalance*. Neither is your condition imagined; it is caused by natural and normal bodily changes that occur in almost all human beings and has an entirely logical explanation. It involves a series of *electrical reactions* in your brain that can be caused by an imbalance. The imbalance can be a result of many things including allergies, energy levels, and stress. The reactions affect every aspect of your bodily functions including all your senses and movements. Most importantly, these electrical reactions in your head can be affected by biochemical messages from other parts of your body – hormones and other substances operating far from your brain.

➢ ELECTRICAL REACTIONS AND PAIN – A METAPHOR

Let us consider a phenomenon called *phantom pain*. This is the case where a soldier, for example, has a hand blown off in a battle. Later, he may feel pain in the missing hand. The pain can be excruciatingly severe. There is no medical explanation for this even though it has been described in the traditional medical literature for centuries. I think I know the source of the phantom pain. I think I understand what is going on in the brain. Not only is it understandable, I think it is treatable in many cases.

Since no one really *knows* what is going on in the brain, I am going to use a simple explanation, a metaphor, that will allow us to imagine an unknown process that might explain what we observe. I will use this simple explanation, not because you might not understand a scientific explanation, but because there isn't one. Remember, traditional medicine has to stop right here. After all, if it isn't in The Book, it does not, *cannot* exist. Medicine doesn't *know* what is going on in your head . . . and neither do I. However, based on what I have observed, based on our tests and the results of treatment success using these observations, I can offer a couple of possible explanations for this phenomenon. It may be due to . . . *increased electrical activity* in the brain. Pain may be due to *increased* electrical activity in the brain.

I think that when the soldier's hand was blown off, the pain receptors in the brain were so sensitized by the injury that the threshold of stimulation was lowered. So, whenever there is an increase in electrical activity in the brain, there may be stimulation of these sensitized pain receptors and the perception of pain begins. The increase in electrical activity may be the result of an imbalance caused by allergy, energy needs, or stress. We will explain this more in detail in later chapters, but when you are low on one or more hormones, your body may respond with ever–increasing amounts of other hormones, adrenalin in particular, and this can cause dramatic increases in the electrical activity in the brain. The result might be pain, as in the case of phantom pain. It could also result in stimulation of outgoing nerve impulses resulting in contraction of muscles, chest tightness, and shortness of breath for example. It could result in rapid heart rate, muscle contraction, and pain, anywhere. It could be severe as in the cases of seizure patients I see, or minimal as in the typical loss of short-term memory. The increase in electrical activity is similar to what you run into when you hit "enter" too often and too fast on your computer; it might jam up and you would have to "re-boot" it. I think the increase in electrical activity can cause a "jam up" in your brain and you may need to "re-boot." I think I can show you how to do that using tiny amounts of hormones placed under your tongue. Any number of symptoms can be caused by this increased electrical activity. You may think of it as "stress"; I think of it as a hormone imbalance. It can be blocked within moments by rebooting your computer (brain) using the hormone drops that we use in our office. We will discuss this in greater detail in Chapter 6 where we refer to this process as "neutralization" or "blocking." The symptoms may be a result of increased electrical activity in the brain and the solution may be as simple as neutralizing that electrical activity with hormone drops. Interestingly enough, in most cases this neutralization will occur almost instantly. Another possibility is that the progesterone drops stimulate a partial agonist effect. It may be that there is an instantaneous blocking of receptor sites by the effect of the dilute progesterone.

➢ THE GOOD NEWS

Is this good news or what?

What if your symptoms really are all in your head? What if that were so even though you don't have any kind of medically recognized disease? Or, if you have been diagnosed with a fatal disease, what if they are wrong? What if the solution were **simple** (drops), **safe** (there has never been a serious reaction to sublingual drops), **effective** (we get rid of over half the symptoms in over half our patients) and **cheap** (we figure the actual cost of the drops is less than $1.00 per month)?

➢ OUR HERITAGE

I have practiced allergy in Austin, Texas since 1985. However, I practice an alternative type of allergy. By searching for the causes of health problems, I treat "mystery diseases." These are called "Category X" disorders by Mariana C. Castells, Associate Professor of Medicine at Harvard Medical School. Testing for hormone reactions is not new. It is done every day at Harvard, at Johns Hopkins, and many other allergy departments. They test for progesterone-mediated inflammation to document things like autoimmune progesterone dermatitis, premenstrual asthma, and premenstrual migraine. They test for it but they do not know how to treat the conditions.

Treating the conditions isn't new. I didn't invent the treatment. It was first described in the literature by Dr. H. Geber in Dermatology Z 1921. He published more findings in the British Journal of Dermatology in 1930, when he wrote of desensitization in the treatment of menstrual intoxication (bad PMS, I guess) and other allergic symptoms. In 1949, Dr. W.E. Phillips described in the Annals of Internal Medicine the successful treatment of pain and asthma symptoms using small amounts of progesterone injected under the skin of patients. Dr. J. B. Miller described the exact same success in the Journal of the Medical Association of the State of Alabama in 1973, again treating patients with pain and asthma using small amounts of injected progesterone. In 1982, my good friend and colleague, Dr. Dick Mabray, published his study in Obstetrics and Gynecology using the same techniques.

Recently, I was meeting with Dr. Mabray and my research associates, Drs. Pat and Dick Richardson of the University of Texas. Dick Richardson and I were getting ready to submit our paper on "Hormone Allergy" ultimately published in the American Journal of Reproductive Immunology. I was complaining about the small number of articles that had ever been printed on the topic. At that point, Dr. Mabray asked if I had seen his paper. I had not. When we looked at it, I was stunned. Everything we set out in our paper had already been done by Dick Mabray and had been published almost 20 years earlier. I was crushed! He had treated all the same kinds of symptoms, pain, shortness of breath, and several others, with the nearly identical percentage of success as I had experienced.

I told Dick how foolish I felt, but he smiled and pointed out what we believe to be a critical difference. My treatment form is sublingual and we proved the existence of *hormone allergy* as the immediate cause of the reactions leading to symptoms. All the earlier work had been done by injection. Injections can be dangerous and they can even cause death by anaphylactic reactions to the antigens. Sublingual is safe. In studies of sublingual antigen use going back to the earliest publications in the 1960's, there has never been a serious reaction to sublingual drops. This is my discovery. It is no invention. It is the discovery, through over 30 years of trials and observations, of a safe, effective, cheap way to treat a wide variety of symptoms.

The only other thing I have added is the possibility that you can do this yourself by putting the tiny doses of progesterone needed to block symptoms in drops you can place under your tongue, as opposed to the traditional method of injecting the same doses under the skin. In most cases, this involves "blocking" progesterone-mediated inflammation to progesterone. I have found this *blocking* or *neutralization* of symptoms to be most effective in the relief of pain and the relief of chest tightness and shortness of breath. However, the progesterone drops are quite effective at relieving symptoms in a variety of areas of discomfort (neck, nose, eyes, throat, ears, skin, back, hips, shortness of breath, headache, and upper and lower extremities).

I find that many disorders respond to sublingual progesterone drops with a significant drop in symptoms, sometimes with complete relief of symptoms, within moments of the placing of the drops under the tongue. The disorders I treat include those listed on the cover of this book.

Additionally, I have been granted a patent for treatment of pain and other progesterone-mediated inflammation related symptoms using dilute hormone solutions (Patent No: US 7,179,798 B2, Feb. 20, 2007). I also have patent applications pending for the following disorders:

1. allergy
2. asthma, shortness of breath, pulmonary fibrosis
3. autoimmune diseases
4. progesterone-mediated inflammation
5. infertility

6. interstitial cystitis
7. macular degeneration
8. multiple sclerosis
9. sinusitis
10. breast cancer
11. polymyositis

This book is not intended to be a scientific resource. I am going to give you a number of possible causes for your health problems, but I will also share with you the possible solutions I have experienced in treating my patients for over 30 years. In brief, here is what this book contains:

1. The most common symptoms
    - Weight Problems
    - Diminished Sex Drive
    - Pain
    - Fatigue
    - Short-term Memory Loss
2. A sampling of first-hand testimonies of individuals who had very similar experiences to those you are having and who have found relief
3. A discussion of *alternative* or *complementary* medical treatment
4. An explanation about the causes of your pain and suffering and how traditional medicine's interpretation of "normal ranges" is misleading
5. A section on hormones and allergies
6. Recommendations for treating your problems with alternative strategies

* (I will use "he" when referring to doctors. I mean no disrespect to all of the wonderful females who are doctors, but I have chosen to use "he" to avoid awkward constructions within the text – i.e., "he or she" or "he/she." "He" should be read as "he or she" throughout.)

Chapter 2

You and Your Symptoms

After 30 years of working in the field of medicine, I have discovered something that causes immediate change in the symptoms that a vast majority of my patients experience. What I have found is that many symptoms occurring in patients are caused by stress. When people get certain symptoms like weight problems, diminished sex drive, pain, fatigue, and short-term memory loss and also like fibromyalgia, arthritis, joint pain, muscle pain, pain in the stomach, pain in the neck, severe headaches, or unexplained shortness of breath, many times these symptoms are caused simply by an imbalance in the patient's systems, most frequently in their hormone systems. Later chapters in this book will explain exactly how these hormones cause these conditions.

The hormones that seem to cause us the most trouble and found in all human beings are DHEA, adrenalin, estrogen, progesterone, testosterone, cortisol, and thyroid. Each of these hormones has its individual purpose and affects bodily functions; however, a single hormone may influence more than one of these functions and each function may be controlled by several hormones. Although we will talk about each of these hormones in detail beginning in Chapter 5, a brief explanation about adrenalin and cortisol is in order because adrenalin causes so many of the problems in most of the patients I see. Cortisol is the hormone we are supposed to use for allergies, energy, and stress. When we get low on cortisol, our body compensates with adrenalin, the hormone that is supposed to be used only for emergencies and high stress situations. What results is that we begin tapping our adrenalin gland for these bursts of energy for every little circumstance that comes along. Soon, not only have we "over-shocked" our system with a stronger chemical than was needed, we have overworked a very important part of our system that has specific and, by design, limited functions. This causes problems across the body and this condition will be referred to later as we talk about the types of symptoms I see most often in the patients who visit my office.

Patients who come to me generally have several types of symptoms. The five that emerge most often in the discussions I have with my patients are *weight problems*, *diminished sex drive*, *pain*, *fatigue*, and *short-term memory loss*.

Weight Problems

Weight reduction and maintenance requires carefully balanced hormones. If we look at the body as a racecar, let's say this racecar has four tires with each tire using a different hormone in it for inflation. We have a high-speed, high-performance racecar here that will do over 200 miles per hour. If one of those tires is down 50% in its pressure (its normal hormone allotment), this car cannot be driven. The tire does not necessarily have to be empty, like medicine thinks; if it is just low, it is not going to perform well. The same is true in human beings. What we usually find is more than just one of the tires is low. The one in the front only has 10% of its normal amount of inflation and the one in the rear has only 50% of its normal inflation; this car is uncontrollable and we are on a very disastrous course. Naturally, the other parts of the car attempt to compensate for this equilibrium imbalance. As a result, we get into this horrendous spin of up–down–up–down with over-corrections and an incredible amount of stress on the driver. Problems of all sorts emerge and tend to bounce off one another until the vehicle overheats and goes into a shutdown mode. This is what happens in the human body as well. Our hormones get out of balance (like the tires) and other parts of our body start trying to compensate.

Our human car has at least seven tires (hormones) instead of four. Problems with weight are likely a result of hormone imbalance. If nature lowers our reproductive hormones (see Ch. 5), then, like neutered farm animals, we will gain weight, mainly fat, in the middle of our bodies. If hormones aren't balanced, we will be like a racecar with a low tire.

Everybody over the last 100 years has been aware of the fact that thyroid may have something to do with weight problems, so the doctor will check their thyroid and then announce to the patient that he or she is normal – or worse yet, will say to the patient, "You are fine." Medicine's point of view is that if you are anywhere within a certain range, you are okay. What they mean to say is *your numbers* fall within *normal limits*. The problem with the way *normal limits* are measured is that the range of normal is much too broad. More will be discussed on this topic in Chapter 5, but right now, take my word for it that what the medical profession uses for *normal* encompasses a number of folks who may be at the 6th percentile of the total range (that means that 94% of the total human population has higher numbers). Additionally, what may be normal for one person may not be normal for the next individual, or at least what level one individual needs to function normally may be an entirely different level for the next person.

There are always other related issues and conditions that are connected to the causes for someone's weight problem, and we do spend considerable time going over these with the patient. But in addition to their weight issues, they are generally going to have the weight–related issues of fatigue, loss of short-term memory, and mood swings (particularly depression). After all, if you are 50 pounds overweight and you cannot find any way to lose the weight, you are going to be depressed. You are generally also going to have diminished sex drive. People who are 20, 30, 40 pounds overweight feel unattractive and this feeling is almost always fed by low hormone levels, one of which is the driving sex hormone, testosterone. The first thing we are going to do with these types of patients is get a blood test and examine the levels of testosterone as well as the other hormones mentioned above. Incidentally, we have not discussed much here in the way of treatment or remedy. Since the treatment for weight issues is similar to sex issues, we will discuss treatment for both in this next section: diminished sex drive.

Diminished Sex Drive

Most people are concerned about sex and they are all mystified why, at age 60, they don't feel like they did when they were 20. What's the mystery here? My attorney recently said, "My doctor says testosterone is bad and he said he does not know what it is going to do to my prostate; testosterone can cause testicular cancer and it can cause prostate cancer." I responded, "Who gets prostate cancer? Old guys. Who has the highest testosterone? Young guys. Now tell me testosterone is bad." In fact, a recent study in England with over 10,000 patients found that men with the highest levels of testosterone had a 41% lower chance of dying from all causes (a huge health factor) than those with lower levels of testosterone. I shared this article with my attorney and he is now taking testosterone. So, testosterone is our friend and we like to have plenty of it around. It is *diminishing* testosterone levels that cause problems, not high ones. Why would anybody be content with normal levels of a 70-year-old? Everyone wants the levels of a 20-year-old if it doesn't do any damage – and it doesn't. Why would we want to put up with that? Do not go quietly "into that dark night."

Most people are having less sex at 50 than they did at 30. Other than one patient (probably lying) who told me sex was better at 60 than it was when he was in his 20's, it just doesn't happen. We have all these changes going on. You are not as limber as you used to be. As a 60-year-old golfer, I don't care how well you hit the ball; you hit it farther when you were 30. All those things are part of the constellation of aging. I am just saying, let's optimize our health rather than accepting old age and aging disorders. Medicine won't pay any attention to someone that is within its notion of "normal" limits.

Many, many patients come to me for no other reason than the fact that their spouses sent them because they "don't have any sex drive." This is a perfectly natural consequence of getting past your 22nd or 23rd birthday. Most of us were howling at the moon in high school and college and the howls got considerably less frequent and much dimmer as we got older. There is pretty good evidence that there is a rather dramatic drop, somewhere between 20–40%, in testosterone in the first 6 months after a man gets married. We think this happens because they are no longer "hunting." Sex is more convenient and so the edge is off; without that edge, there is less testosterone production. This continues into middle age and beyond to the point where we may not completely lose our sex drive, but it is surely subdued. Much of this is due to this drop in testosterone.

I was married at 20 and we had two children by the time I was 22. In my 23rd year, I gained 75 pounds for no apparent reason. I didn't do anything different; I was eating the same food, doing the same exercise, and I was just stacking on the weight. I couldn't believe my eyes, and I cared much less about sex. So, here I am at 23 and I have discovered that I am going to have to start running one to two hours a day and eating a very low calorie diet, mainly eating protein, and that helped me keep my weight steady as long as I did it seven days a week. I didn't know anything about the hormones and wasn't practicing medicine at that time. I was a young lawyer running all day long trying to fit into my pants, but it was really clear to me that something dramatic had happened to my sex drive. This was a little mystifying because I had been rather committed to that as a younger man and newly married.

Nevertheless, I run into more and more people who for one reason or another realize that something strange has happened to their sex drive in their lives. This is particularly true of 40-year-old women, and the problem, as I see it, goes back to the hormone imbalance. We find a lady who, because of her adrenal state and hormone imbalance, has gained 20, 30, or 40 pounds. First of all, she is going to feel terribly unattractive. She steps out of the shower in the morning and she looks and thinks that this is the most disgusting thing she has ever seen. I frequently ask her if her husband feels the same way and the response is usually, "Oh, he thinks I look great, but he is just a man." I say, "So my problem then is you. As far as I know, most guys are pretty much straight line thinkers. He thinks you look just as good as you ever did, but you don't agree with him, and you think he is a little nutty because he can't see how disgusting you look." Most women generally agree with this summation of the situation.

I say to them, "So, our problem then is that you have two children, you work all day, you come home at night, and you have to feed the children. You are so tired you can hardly move, at which point your husband comes home, pats you on the bottom, and says 'Hi honey, how about dinner?'" At which point you are ready to knock his head off because he can't see how tired you are or how upset you are. Guys and their sex drive are pretty much always on "go" (those whose testosterone level is not in the closet), and I am sure you look just as good to him as the day he married you. More importantly, you are feeling less and less inclined to have sex, which makes him more and more driven to try and get sex, because everybody wants what they can't have. This has become some treasure that he keeps trying to get and we run into the situation where the wife is afraid to give the husband a kiss on the cheek or a pat on the butt because he might mistakenly think she feels friendly, and she doesn't. Her body thinks she is being chased by the mad dogs and hungry bears of everyday life, and nobody stops to make love when mad dogs and hungry bears are right behind them. He is beginning to get resentful because he thinks she doesn't love him as much as she used to and all guys take this very personally. If the wife doesn't respond to the husband, then the husband thinks he is making a "D" in sex, so he is all the more driven to try and prove himself.

➢ NATURAL HORMONE FLUCTUATIONS

In addition to all of these psychological issues that are flying around, there are some physical changes going on as well. As women get older and their hormones change, there is a thinning of vaginal tissue, and this thinning produces dryness. Intercourse, which used to be so pleasurable both emotionally and physically, now hurts. So, we now have a situation where the lady feels unattractive because of the weight gain. She feels like she is being chased by bears because she runs on adrenalin. She has a resentful, pouty husband that wants sex. When she finally gives in to the whining, the sex isn't very satisfying . . . and it *hurts.* With these conditions, sex isn't going to happen very often, and the less often it happens, the more her body is convinced that she is a little old lady – so the body makes even fewer sex hormones. The whole thing is "heading south."

There are, however, some happy solutions to this. Most of these women are spiritually oriented folks, and our conversation goes something like this. "Do you believe that God loves you?" "Yes, He does." "Well, does He love you just like you are at this weight?" "Oh yes, He loves me." "Does your husband love you?" "Yes, he loves me." "Does he object to your weight?" Occasionally some beast of a husband will complain about the weight, but typically, she will say, "No, he thinks I look great." "Then we really only have one problem, don't we? You are tougher than God, and you are being more critical of yourself than God or your husband. This is sort of an arrogant position to take in life, and we are not going to make any progress as long as you maintain this attitude."

I point out to these women that the program of recovery from this point has many facets, and basically what we need to do will require some time. I ask them to suspend judgment for 60 days and try to get past this overpowering need to lose 20 pounds by next Friday night. We have to understand that this is going to take some time. In the meantime, the only way it is ever going to work is if they can get over this feeling of self-disgust, this contempt for themselves. "You have to accept yourself just the way you are. If you can accept that, then we have the possibility of change. If you can't, you keep yourself under such enormous pressure that no change will be possible."

Let me use the example of athletes. If I were to tell a champion baseball player that if he did not hit the next ball out of the ballpark, I was going to shoot him in the foot. He would not even see the ball. There would be so much pressure he wouldn't be able to function at all. We have to first relieve the pressure. I know this takes a great act of faith on her part, but I tell her that she is going to be with this guy another 30 or 40 years, assuming she has a good relationship and she loves her husband. We really don't have any choice. You have to try something different; nothing that you have tried has worked. There is no pill that will make you well. There is no diet that will make you well. All diets work while we diet, but as soon as we slow down the diet, get bored with it, or stop losing weight, then we go right back to where we were because we have to change the way we eat, change the hormone balance in our bodies, change the way we behave, and get into activities that promote weight loss.

➢ RESTORING BALANCE

The first thing we are going to do is draw blood and find out which of the tires on our hormone racecar are low. Invariably, we find that the thyroid is low, the estrogen is low, and the DHEA (another fairly active hormone) is low. You might have a high testosterone level (probably one in 100 that I see does), but if you are running on adrenalin, you are going to be too frazzled and too stressed to use it. Not all women need testosterone added, but almost every patient I see is going to be low in some aspect in her thyroid, her estrogen, or her DHEA. You are highest in your hormones for the five years after you begin menstruating and most of you started between ages 13 to

18. Then, things begin to happen and none of them are good. As soon as you have a baby, nature is going to slam your hormones through the floor. That is the way nature makes sure you don't have a baby every nine months. When a baby is born, all the sex hormones go down for about two years until the nursing is over, allowing the body to recover to have another one. So, if you have had three or four babies, I imagine there has been constant weight gain since the second or third baby, constant diminishment of the sex drive, and constant increase in stress in your life. I cannot tell you how many patients I see that are stressed to the max because they have three small children at home, a large child for a husband, a dog, a car, and a house that they have to take care of and – on top of all of this – diminishing hormones. This is an impossible situation. They are doing three full time jobs and wonder why they feel tired.

So, our first step on the road to recovery is to get the hormones back where they need to be. We will frequently have these patients wear a pulse meter (found at any athletic store) around their chest so they have some instrument that tells them when they are in the adrenalin range (stressing) during the day. When we are stressed, our body puts out adrenalin; and when we put out adrenalin (which for people with a hormone imbalance is about every two hours), the blood sugar drops like a rock. Then, they have to squirt out another dose of adrenalin. They will crave carbohydrates because adrenalin can only use carbohydrate for fuel. As a result, these people are running on adrenalin every two hours, each excursion a little lower than the previous one, so that by the end of the day they are so tired they can't move. Yet, that is the time when they are going to go home and face three hungry children, a husband, and a dog. No wonder they are tired.

I try to put their hormones back in balance so they are less likely to need adrenalin to deal with their allergies, energy needs, and stress. I also give them a pulse meter so they can see, before they put out the adrenalin, when they are getting close. We can avoid the adrenalin rush if we know it is coming. For example, if your husband was fond of jumping out from behind a door and startling you on a dark night as you came in, you wouldn't be able to sleep the rest of the night. You would be so adrenalized and upset. Suppose we put a little device on your wrist so that when you got out of the car it began to beep and said, "Jack is hiding behind the door." You wouldn't be frightened at all, and that is what the pulse meter does. It tells you *before* you squirt out adrenalin what is coming. Once the adrenalin begins, it is too late; nobody can stop it. Your brain can be completely calm, and you realize everything is all right in the world regardless how it might seem, but your body is not listening. It is a prehistoric piece of equipment and when it squirts out adrenalin, it takes your brain along with it. But if you knew the adrenalin was coming, then you could override the hormone reaction. We can talk to our own adrenals and say, "Jack is hiding behind the door. Let's go say 'hello' to him." It won't be scary and that works. You can look at your pulse meter, stare at it, and watch your pulse come down just by being aware of that potential adrenalin rush.

➢ DIET AND STRESS

In addition to removing stress, we want patients to change their diet. Diet change is very difficult. I have been on every diet known to man in my life because I have had this weight problem since I was 23. All diets work for us as long as we "work" the diet. On the other hand, if people want to have relations with their spouse after a Friday evening dinner, then they had better pay close attention to their diet *because it influences their sex drive*. If you go out and have a big bowl of pasta or a pizza, and drink a pitcher of beer, you may be taken home in a wheelbarrow. There will not be any sex. So, if you are serious about having an intimate relationship, then you have to do the things that promote that relationship. Maybe if you are going out on a date with your spouse, you just have a salad and you only drink water. After you have sex, then you can have some pizza, pasta, and a glass of beer or wine or something, but we have to figure out the things that work for the relationship and the things that don't.

Relationships require nurture, hormones, low stress, and diet. Getting hormones back to higher levels will help, but more sex drive is not going to hit you over the head like it did when you were in college. It is very easy to put testosterone back into a person's life and that will help. But unless we get rid of that adrenalin, nothing is going to work very well. You won't feel like having sex when the bears are chasing you down the street no matter how high your testosterone is.

We try to reduce the need for adrenalin by balancing the hormones. We increase the sex hormones when necessary and we try to eat a diet that doesn't provoke things that can cause adrenalin surges of things that wire us up. This would be stuff like caffeine, chocolate, and sugar. A coke would be a good example.

Adrenalin can burn only carbohydrates for fuel, so all these patients are sugar addicts, all of them, without exception. They may say, "Oh, I don't eat sugar." I ask them what they do eat. The response: "Fruit." I tell them fruit is sugar; maybe not sugar exactly, but carbohydrates are close enough and they include the sugars, of course. They say, "Bread or chips." I tell them that it is carbohydrate, too. The only things that are not carbohydrate are fish, fowl, and meat. Everything else has carbohydrate in it and some are more dangerous than others. Obviously, Coca-Cola or caffeine could be serious causes of adrenalin release. The faster we can absorb a sugar, the more likely we will react by releasing adrenalin. So liquids would be a fast-acting form of sugar. An apple can be fast, medium, or slow. Apple juice is fast. It goes right across the tummy, gets them wired up, and folks like it because it fuels their adrenalin. Coca-Cola, apple juice, fruit juice, quick sugars, chocolate . . . these things are the most likely to fuel adrenalin surges. And remember, if you are running on adrenalin, you need a dose of your carbohydrate (sugar) about every two to three hours or you will feel a hypoglycemic shakiness.

➢ MOVEMENT AND LSD

So, there are things we can do to modify our diet so that we don't run into these big swings of mood that follow the adrenalin's up and down jolts of energy. We have the patients use the pulse meter devices to help avoid the episodes of adrenalin, but the final and probably most important thing we want people to do is *get rid* of adrenalin through *movement*. Many patients I see are dedicated exercise people. Some of them actually have trainers, some are marathon runners, and some are kick boxers. The reason that is not working for any of my patients is that they are up into the range of exercise that stimulates adrenalin, which is the opposite of what they are needing. If you have a hormone imbalance, it is very easy for your body to put out adrenalin. As soon as you start putting out adrenalin, you stop burning fat and your blood sugar drops. We are talking about how they can improve their life by diminishing the *intensity* of their exercise.

Frank Shorter, the famous running guru, advocated using LSD years ago and it was a real attention-grabbing headline. By LSD, he meant *long slow distance*. Every time we move a muscle, slowly, we use up a unit of adrenalin. One fast jolt of movement and we put out enough adrenalin to light up a house for the next several hours, and there is no fat burning from that point forward for four to six hours. However, if the body starts moving slowly and it is not startled, and it is not putting out adrenalin, it will use fat for fuel. The chart below shows the different heart rate levels for different types of exercise; these are posted in every gym on earth. It is well known that there are three distinct ranges of exercise:

- fat burning range
- cardiovascular range
- athletic training range

TRAINING HEART RATE

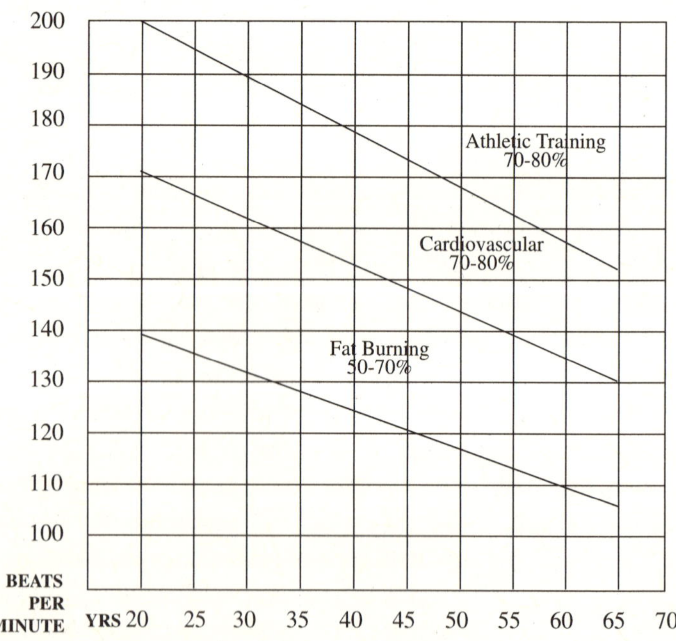

(*Note: These lines represent the averages of the indicated ranges.)

Any time we get above the fat burning range, we are into adrenalin. It is called *fat burning* because we can only burn fat when there is no adrenalin. If we can move slowly for an extended period of time in the fat burning range, then the body realizes there is no emergency and it will use the most efficient fuel for that, which is fat. Any hint of an emergency and it stops burning fat for several hours and starts using blood sugar, its *emergency* fuel.

➢ SLOW MOVEMENT BURNS FAT

My point is this. If I could get my patients to move slowly for an extended period of time burning only fat, then like a large inertia wheel the body will continue to burn fat afterward for several hours so long as they don't put out adrenalin. The best time for this movement is one hour just before they go to sleep, because if they go to sleep, then there won't be any emergency, there won't be any adrenalin put out, and as a result they will probably burn fat all through the night. Dr. Ken Cooper who runs the Cooper Clinic in Dallas, Texas, is a famous cardiologist who was in the Air Force when I was in medical school. I did medicine rotations under him, and he had this wonderful plan for cardiovascular health: exercise and diet. We were told the Air Force fired him, kicked him out, because the generals did not want to hear that they weren't supposed to smoke or drink and that they should start exercising; that was considered heresy. In their minds, heart problems were to be dealt with using medication or surgery. I was very impressed with Dr. Cooper's views on exercise. Dr. Cooper really believed in *vigorous* exercise, which led me to run one to two hours a day at a really fast pace for so many years that I destroyed my feet and my knee and my hip. Today, he suggests more moderate exercise; in fact, he now *walks* one hour daily.

So, Dr. Cooper has changed his mind about the intensity of the exercise. We use this example. If you put $100 in the Dr. Roby's savings bank, he will give you 4% interest. If you put $200 in the Dr. Roby's savings bank he will give you 24% interest, six times as much. By this, we mean that if you *walk slowly* for 30 minutes (the $100), it will increase your rate of fat burning three-fold. You will burn three times more fat, and that will continue for three and a half to four hours after you do the exercise. If you do that for 60 minutes, you will increase your fat burn three fold and it can last up to 24 hours. Knowing that, how could anybody stop at the end of 30 minutes? The big payoff is in the second 30 minutes because we start that inertia wheel going that burns fat, and the longer we do it, the longer the wheel turns. *I cannot urge everybody strongly enough to make up their minds that they will do at least 30 minutes before going to bed.* It seems manageable. But I know perfectly well if they do 30 minutes, I am really hoping that their brain will kick in and they will say the big payoff is in the next 30 minutes. They will be going so slowly that nobody is going to get tired doing it; nobody is going to get breathless. On a treadmill, this is two and a half to three miles per hour, which is practically a stroll.

➢ FAT BURNING HEART RATE

Everybody thinks that if the fat burning level is about 60% of maximum heart rate and cardiovascular is about 70% and athletic is about 90%, then they assume that this translates into Fat Burning Level 1, Fat Burning Level 2, and Fat Burning Level 3. It absolutely does NOT mean that, unless you are Lance Armstrong or some perfectly balanced Olympic athlete. If you are a serious athlete, then yes, the more you go, the more fat you will burn; but that is just not true for most of us. For most of us, we start getting into adrenalin well before we reach mid-levels. Even on your treadmill, there is a "Fat Burning" or "Weight" range displayed, and if you exceed it, it will indicate you are out of the fat burning range. All these gyms are filled with people who are rippling with muscles, still have a fat belly or a fat butt, and they are beside themselves. They cannot figure out how to get rid of it. I see it all the time at the gym. These are enormously powerful people because they are happy to do the high levels of exercise. But it is really hard to wrap our heads around the idea that low-level exercise might be more effective. Slower might be better than faster. We have to define our goal. If your goal is to qualify for the Senior Olympics, then get up to the top range and stay there. If you are concerned about your heart, then you need to be in the middle range, the cardiovascular range. I do athletic training every morning. If I want to lose weight, have sex drive, and live a more fulfilling life, I'm into LSD (long, slow distance).

➢ FAST, MEDIUM, SLOW

I like going fast; I have always liked going fast. In the mornings, I just go all out and get my heart rate up to about 170. I am currently 67 years old, so that is 20 or 30 beats more than where I ought to have it for any reasonable level, but I like that and my heart is capable of it. In the afternoon, I generally play racquetball and my heart rate range is 120 to 140; the exercise is fairly vigorous. It takes my breath away and I am dripping with perspiration. After that, I typically do an hour of Pilates three or four times a week, which is slow but intense exercise. BUT, I always try for seven nights a week on my treadmill before bed; like everyone else who sets goals, this means I may actually hit five, but almost always I am going to do an hour to an a hour and a half on the treadmill just before I go to sleep at a real slow heart rate (no higher than 90) watching old DVD movies that won't startle me so that I can rest. The *only* reason I am doing that treadmill is so my pants will fit. I am not worried about my heart. I have lots of fun; I do the fast exercise in the morning because I enjoy going fast; I do the racquetball in the afternoon because I love to do it; I do the slow walking late in the evening so I can rest. I will go deeply asleep, and I will rest and wake up refreshed; but most importantly, my pants will fit.

➢ ADRENALIN INCREASES WEIGHT

If we are interested in losing weight, we have to get rid of adrenalin. If we are interested in a sexually fulfilling relationship, we have to get rid of adrenalin. Whatever our goal is, adrenalin is our enemy, and the best way to get rid of adrenalin is long, slow distance, just before we go to sleep. There is a rumor that sex relieves adrenalin, and that is often true. It seems to be typically so for younger men. They have sex, they are knocked out, and they go fast asleep. However, about 40% of the women I see are agitated after sex; for them we recommend sex in the morning so that it doesn't interfere with their sleep. We point out that sex, as a means of releasing adrenalin, is probably most effective when we are 20-year-old newlyweds. It becomes less and less effective as we get older. My treadmill is a much more dependable method for reducing adrenalin . . . not as much fun, of course, but quite dependable.

There is a lot of stuff even now by the AMA and by the health institutes talking about how you will feel better if you go slower, but they are not providing the explanation as to why you are going to feel worse if you go faster. I need patients to get rid of adrenalin so there is some possibility of fat burning, for better sex, for less pain, for more rest, and for less fatigue. Adrenalin aggravates whatever is wrong with you; adrenalin is a *major* cause of problems in the body. A diminished sex drive may be the result of adrenalin. Few of us feel like making love when we feel like our life is being threatened due to an over-sensitive or exhausted adrenal gland. I can't put a gun between your eyes and say, "Do it" and expect a happy result. This topic of reducing adrenalin output involves all five of our most common symptoms.

Pain

Much of what we recommend for women who come into our offices revolves around the issues just discussed: balancing hormones, reducing stress, changing our diet, and incorporating exercise into our daily regimen. However, even though weight problems and diminished sex drive are important to mental health, pain will get your attention more quickly than anything else. In Chapter 6, we will provide a more detailed explanation of how we deal with symptoms of pain and how that works, but in order to understand how we treat pain in the section below, we need to discuss briefly our methods.

The process that we use in my office is different from what is done in anyone else's office. We *block* or *neutralize* symptoms. When I say *neutralize*, I mean we interrupt whatever the irritation is that is causing the symptoms, whether it be pain, shortness of breath, itching, or any other discomforting symptom. We do that by introducing a tiny amount of the substance that we think is causing the problem. In the most general of terms, this follows the principles of homeopathy that was first used in the late 1700s and early 1800s in Germany but now finds its widest base of application in Great Britain. Its use in Europe has been going on for over 150 years, but the center of homeopathy at this time is found in Great Britain. Homeopathy involves the principle of finding the offending substance and using weaker and weaker amounts of that same substance to first cause an increase in the symptoms and then to diminish or stop the symptoms in the patient.

However, we skip a step. We find what the offending agent is and go straight to *blocking* the symptoms. So that now when a new patient comes into my office, we try a variety of substances. We have also come around to the European and British type of testing and treatment, which is done with sublingual drops. Sublingual drops are drops of solution that are placed under the tongue. We ask the patient to let it sit there for five seconds and then they swallow; 10 or 15 seconds after that, they can generally tell some change in their symptoms. This happens so fast that it is completely unexplainable by conventional knowledge of how our bodies function.

Everything in medicine presumes that if we put medicine in your mouth, it has to go to your stomach, then into your blood stream, and it then has to circulate around the body. This takes a considerable amount of time before it can have any effect on the pain in your leg or your head or your shortness of breath. On the other hand, if we put something in intravenously, if we inject something right into a patient's vein, then the only limitation on time is how long it takes something to get around the body in one cycle of the circulation system. For example, if we inject a bitter flavored drug into somebody's arm and it is pumped around the body, we measure how long it takes until you can taste it. That is a rough approximation of circulation time and it takes roughly a minute. The very quickest anything could conceivably happen in traditional medical thinking is in "circulation time"; that is to say, it takes at least a minute for any substance to have an effect. When we discovered that patients can see a dramatic change in their symptoms in less than 15 seconds, this means that we are into some unknown territory. I suggest this instantaneous reaction might be explained as a type of *neurohumoral transmission* (n*euro* – nerves or electronics; *humoral* – blood or circulatory system). This simply means that we think the substance under the tongue triggers a nerve reaction instantly so that the patient can see a difference within 10 to 15 seconds. We have actually done tests on patients who were known to react to a substance. We measured their brain waves, using an electroencephalogram. We found that the patient can feel a difference in 10 to 15 seconds, but the electroencephalogram showed a dramatic increase in alpha brain waves in less than one second from the time we put the substance under their tongue. Speaking of pain, let's talk about patients who are not overweight or who have diminished sex drive, but who experience varying degrees of pain on a daily basis.

➢ PAIN DOCTORS – FIBROMYALGIA

The most frequent referrals I get are from traditional physicians known as "pain doctors." They send me patients who typically are suffering from what medicine refers to as *fibromyalgia*. The word fibromyalgia means "muscle soreness" (*fibro* – connective tissue; *myalgia* – pain or soreness). Medicine frequently uses technical words to describe simple symptoms of which the patient already is aware. Fibromyalgia patients have been recognized as having this well-known syndrome, a constellation of symptoms, that fits a fairly rigid definition as set out by the American College of Rheumatology. We have many *syndromes* like that; for example, a gastroenterologist will frequently tell patients that they have IBS (irritable bowel syndrome). What they are telling the patients, in effect, is that they have a stomachache, and they then do extensive testing. They run tubes down the patients' throats and up their bottoms and the conclusion always has to do with cellular changes and things like that. Yet these kinds of disorders have been recognized for 2000 years and they are known to be related to food. Medicine has been pointing out that "One man's food is another man's poison" for a couple of thousand years. The food is not mentioned; however, it is the most likely *cause* of the problem. Likewise, in the pain patients, the hormones are not mentioned either, because this is not what we were taught in medical school. And yet, a hormone imbalance or progesterone-mediated inflammation may well be the *cause* of the pain.

Pain doctors are seeing many patients who have vague pains in several parts of their bodies. The thing that makes it difficult for the doctor to accept is the fact that the pain changes from day to day, joint to joint. On Monday, the left shoulder might hurt. Using a scale of pain from 0 (no pain at all) to 10 (the worst pain they ever experienced), then these patients frequently come in with pain ranging from 5 to 10. It is very serious, debilitating pain; they cannot work; they cannot lift that arm or leg. But the peculiar thing is that Tuesday it might be the right shoulder, and Wednesday it might be the left knee. The pain moves all over the body. The patient cannot isolate the pain; it moves around! Doctors would be happy if they could find a lesion on the head of the femur (thighbone) and say, "Oh, you have a lesion on the head of the femur; we can remove it and your pain will be resolved." But this is not the case at all. This pain moves all over the place and it is not necessarily in the joints; sometimes it is in the muscles leading up to the joints. The clinical definition of fibromyalgia requires the patient to have somewhere around 17 different points of tenderness and/or pain. To qualify for fibromyalgia, you have to jump through a pretty tiny hoop. Nevertheless, many patients who have joint pain are told by their physician that they have fibromyalgia, which is an accurate enough description because they do indeed have pain. But this kind of pain can be so severe it is often not relieved by serious narcotics. The pain doctors' clinics are basically filled with patients who have unexplained pain; if it were explainable, then the doctor could probably do something about it.

Traditional medicine is really good at detecting and treating known diseases, broken bones, and things like that. But these pains we are talking about are vague and there is no known disease that involves moving pain. The patients may tell the doctors these pains are worse the week before their menstrual period. It seems to be perfectly clear to female patients that the problem has to do with their hormones. Doctors do not acknowledge this because we were not taught that in medical school. As a result, the doctor is dealing with a patient who has moderate-to-severe pain that moves around with varying intensity from day to day or week to week and is not relieved by narcotics. This is not a happy situation. The patients are very demanding; they want relief. They want stronger and stronger pain medication. The doctors are more and more reluctant to give it to them because they are worried about creating a dependence situation where they have a drug addict on their hands and the pain is still not relieved. These are the doctors who will say, "Why don't you go see Dr. Roby?" They know I do not use any kind of narcotics; we do not even use pain medication. I am going to try to block the *cause* of the pain and, while the pain doctor may not understand that, it relieves him of this burdensome patient who is getting increasingly agitated over the doctor's inability to relieve her pain.

➢ PAIN RELIEF – SUBLINGUAL DROPS

It has been our experience in dealing with hormone imbalance and neutralizing symptoms using the sublingual drops that all manner of pain is relieved. When I see new patients with severe pain, in three cases out of four, we can give them 75–85% relief of all their pain within the first 15 minutes of working with them.

We do this by blocking the cause of the pain, which in my view is most often an allergic reaction to some type of hormone or stress reaction. But all of these reactions are mediated by the hormone adrenalin, and if I can find the cause of the adrenalin release and block that, then there will be a nearly instantaneous relief of their pain. When we do that, we have done a couple of things.

First of all, we relieve the pain. The patients are very grateful. They are shocked. They are surprised, and then they get angry with their doctors because they did not do that. We explain that he does not know how to do this. He did exactly what he was trained to do and this is something new and different and it works; it works very effectively most of the time. It does not work in every case. If the treatment does not work, there is no charge at all. If it does work, and they for some reason are still dissatisfied with the treatment, we offer a full money-back guarantee at any time. We know the patient is going to have to do a large number of things to make this continue to work. All I am going to do is give them some immediate relief of the pain, which shows them the pain can be relieved by blocking the *cause* of the pain. If I put drops under their tongue that blocks the pain reaction, the pain goes away instantly. There is some possibility the pain may not return at least until they get back into the situation that caused the adrenalin to be released in the first place.

Let's consider the example of someone who is startled. Suppose you see a ghost (or think you do). The back of your neck is going to get tight and all the classic symptoms like feeling as if your heart is going to jump out of your chest. We would see rapid heart rate (tachycardia). "I couldn't get my breath. I felt like I was going to choke." The chest gets tight because of the adrenalin. "I couldn't swallow." The throat gets very tight when people release the adrenalin, so they have difficulty swallowing. The most common symptom, however, is tightness in the back of the neck. Everybody who has had biology remembers the examples of reflexes. If we touch a hot stove, we do not have to think about it; an electrical signal goes from the fingers to the spinal cord and it causes an instantaneous jerk of the hand to pull it away from the pain. We do not have to think about that; it is an automatic *reflex*. The most primitive reflex in all creatures with a spinal cord involves the neck. If we start releasing adrenalin (shooting a gun off close by), the head will snap down on our neck. The same thing will occur in a grass snake, a turtle, a duck, or a human.

➢ ADRENALIN – LITTLE GUNSHOTS

My patients are hearing little gunshots going off in their heads all day long. This may be due to stress, airborne allergy, progesterone-mediated inflammation, food allergy, or energy demands. Adrenalin is released and this pulls the neck down tighter and tighter onto their shoulders, so that the most common pain I run into is neck and shoulder pain. From there, it spreads on down the back. As I am sitting talking to patients, I watch them reach up with their hands and slowly rub the back of their necks, and I realize that even as I am speaking, I am causing them some agitation. Maybe they are getting excited about what I am saying, but their neck is getting tighter. We try to point out to patients that if they have a hormone imbalance, their body is going to release adrenalin. It might be due to low cortisol, or because they are low on testosterone, or because they are low on estrogen. This happens to all of us over the age of 20. If any of these hormones are low and the body starts putting out adrenalin, then it does not matter whether it is bad news or good news; almost anything at all causes us to put out adrenalin. Adrenalin is going to make whatever is wrong with you worse, and it will do so right away.

➢ PHANTOM PAIN

This is why old Aunt Emma can always tell that it is going to rain three days before the rain gets here; her knee starts to hurt. It does that because Aunt Emma injured that knee when she was a little girl and that part of her brain was sensitized by that injury. Now these sensitized pain receptors fire off before other areas of the brain, because there is a lower threshold of excitation. Aunt Emma's body, before the rainstorm, notices that there is a change in barometric measure. A weather front coming through causes a change in barometric pressure. This change causes mold to sporulate (produce spores) at night. When the mold count goes up, Aunt Emma's body tries to release cortisol. Since she has been out of cortisol many years, she instead starts putting out adrenalin. Adrenalin rings the bell of those sensitized pain receptors and her knee starts hurting all over again like it did the first time. Then, a separate part of her brain sends out protective signals, trying to hold the knee in a comfortable position. As a result, she gets muscle soreness and swelling in the area. The brain also causes the area in the knee to release protective chemicals, like histamines, which cause it to turn red and feel hot, swollen, and sore. All this is happening not because of anything going on in the knee, but because she released adrenalin in response to mold, and her brain responded to the adrenalin with activation of the sensitized pain receptors. The result is severe knee pain, which is a result of this cascade of events. But remember: there is nothing going on in her knee to cause this. It is all occurring in her brain. This is *phantom pain*.

➢ PAIN – ALL IN YOUR HEAD

When people get fibromyalgia and the pain moves around their body, they are releasing adrenalin and different areas of the body get tight. If you hold something long enough or tight enough, you are going to have serious pain. Try an experiment: hold up a gallon of milk straight out to your side parallel to the floor as long as you can. You will have the most intense pain you can imagine, because as that area gets tighter and tighter from the stress of trying to hold that muscle, your body releases adrenalin and this makes everything get terribly tight. Even when you release the weight, you will have soreness and some pain for several hours afterward. Females are familiar with the phenomenon as it just happens to women more frequently than men. A little bit of pain at first, and then a little more pain, and finally they are all bound up in pain and they go to the doctor and the doctor gives them that worst of all possible news, "There is nothing wrong with you." Well, now we have somebody that is not only in pain but is seriously ticked off. "What, do think I'm imagining this pain?" That is sort of the impression that we doctors are giving: this is all in your head. The problem is that they are describing the pain without really understanding its cause. They are saying it is imagined; it is not. But it *is* in your head.

After all, your brain is in your head and if the brain is affected by adrenalin, then all hell breaks loose down below. We get neck tightness, shoulder pain, stomach pain, frequency of urination, ovarian pain, swelling in the breasts, tenderness in the breasts before and after periods . . . pain all over the body. This is what frustrates the doctor and the patient; there does not seem to be any rhyme or reason for the pain . . . unless we look for a central cause. If we look for a central cause, this gets easy.

If somebody goes and walks three or four hours slowly in a very quiet park, their pain will diminish. In fact, I tell all my patients that I can cure all their pain in one month. All I need them to do is go take a job as a fly fishing guide in Wyoming, and within 30 days they will have no pain whatsoever and they will sleep like a baby every night. Of course, their husbands will be home with the crying kids and a screaming baby, but they probably won't have any pain. Our evidence for this is that when patients do get calm, and when they are able to go on vacation, and when Grandma does take care of the kids for the weekend, all the pain seems to subside. However, all we need to do is have Grandma bring the kids back on Sunday night, the husband complain about the dinner, or have somebody cut in front of her in traffic, and we are right back where we started . . . sudden, sharp pain. Her stomach is upset, she feels like she is going to throw up, and she feels like she has to urinate immediately. All this because of a jolt of adrenalin.

We have the same amount of cortisol (the hormone we are supposed to use for allergies, energy, and stress) as prehistoric man. Can you imagine a Neanderthal riding down the freeway with you in your SUV? He would dissolve in a puddle of pee on the floor. He would be overwhelmed by the stress. The problem is that we have the same amount of cortisol as he did. There was never any evolutionary pressure to make more cortisol; anybody who did not have enough, died before they were old enough to have children. We enter the 21st Century with the same amount of cortisol as people from hundreds of thousands of years ago and yet an enormously increased amount of stress. Anytime we run out of cortisol and start using adrenalin, we are going to have a problem.

Everything we are going to talk about having to do with pain, weight problems, sex drive, loss of short-term memory, and fatigue, has to do with adrenalin. The sooner we find ways to get rid of the adrenalin or control its output and balance our hormones, the sooner we can resolve these problems. These same patients who have trouble with pain are going to be the first ones who get up in the morning feeling terribly tired because they did not rest well at night. When they wake up and they are terribly tired, what are they going to do? They have been out of cortisol for a long time. So, they are going to stop at Starbucks and get a powerful cup of coffee, which is going to give them a huge jolt of adrenalin first thing in the morning. Two hours later, the adrenalin has subsided, and they need another jolt of adrenalin. This goes on all day long, day after day. When they fall asleep at night, they are unable to sleep deeply enough to get to the fourth level of sleep. As a result, they don't get *rest.*

➢ ADRENALIN AND REST

When we go to sleep at night, we go through several stages of sleep and the deepest one (rapid eye movement or REM sleep) occurs after we have been asleep for about 90 minutes. This is the one that gives us rest and allows recovery of all the systems in our body. Very few people over the age of about 18 or 20 experience this deepest level of sleep, this restful sleep, or REM sleep, on a regular basis. There are a couple of stages before this that are also required for rest but most of my patients never get down to the third or fourth level of sleep. They are sleeping very lightly, easily awakened by any tick or click in the house, and many patients wake up frequently during the night and have to urinate. This is a result of low cortisol. They run on adrenalin all day, which is very much like drinking coffee all day. If you drank two cups of coffee every hour until you went to sleep, you would not rest well at night. Most people put out enough adrenalin to equal the effect of having way too much coffee. As a result, they may lie awake at night, trying to go to sleep, and when they go to sleep, they do not get asleep deeply enough to rest. Or they fall asleep in complete exhaustion at 8 or 9 o'clock at night as soon as they lay their head down, but they are simply exhausted by the use of adrenalin all day and they are not anywhere near a deep enough level of sleep to actually *rest*. Consequently, they sleep lightly during the night because they are so highly adrenalized all day and every morning they are going to wake up with the same feeling that they have not had enough rest. Day by day, they are going to get more tired, eventually reaching complete exhaustion. They are going to have to use more adrenalin to get through their next day, and before long, we have somebody who is in severe pain, chronic fatigue, and/or adrenal exhaustion and whose doctor says there is nothing wrong with them.

➢ BRAIN SWELLING

To give you an example, let us suppose for a moment that I wanted to make you unconscious. To do that, I will want to make your brain swell. If I am allowed to do anything I want to you, I would wrap a rope around your ankles and haul you upside down so that your head is down and your feet are up in the air. If we did that, before several minutes, you would be unconscious because of the pooling of blood in your head. This would cause your two frontal brain hemispheres to swell and disconnect, and you would be unconscious. If I could not hang you upside down but I still wanted to make your brain swell, I would do the next best thing: I would lay you flat on a surface. If I lay you flat, it might take a little longer, but your nose will stop up, you will have difficulty breathing, and your brain will still swell. Most of us experience this because we cannot sleep flat on a mattress; if I tried that, my nose would stop up. I have to use one or two pillows to prop my head up, just so I can breathe at night.

Now, if hanging you upside down were the worst thing and laying you flat is the next worse, what would the *best* thing be to prevent swelling? Obviously, it would be standing you upright; but if I do that, you still will not be alert because your brain has bypass mechanisms. If your brain is swollen and I stand you upright, the blood will just go around the swollen cortex. We have bypass mechanisms in the brain that allow blood to go around a swollen area. So, not only do I need to get you upright . . . I need to increase the fluid flow *through* your brain, so that I can force some of this congestion and swelling that takes place in your cortex to go away; we are going to show you how to do that with *pumps*.

The main pump in your body is your heart; that is our primary pump but it is not nearly big enough to do what I have in mind. In order to pump the fluid through your body and make you feel better, clear your head up, and get rid of the fatigue, we have to engage the really big pumps. Those are the ones in your legs and your arms, and that is why I want people to get upright and walk slowly to start moving fluid around the body to reduce the swelling in your brain, so you can feel better and feel less fatigued. I want to convince patients to try this before they go to sleep, to tell themselves they are *not* tired, they just *feel* tired. They are going to try this experiment for 30 days. If they do that and if they move slowly, they will feel so much more rested and relaxed that they will be able to get deeply asleep, waking up needing much less adrenalin the next morning.

➢ HOW CORTISOL WORKS

We talked above about the fact that we have the same amount of cortisol as prehistoric man. I was told in medical school that all humans use *all* of their cortisol every day. Cortisol comes from the adrenal glands, and it is what we are supposed to use for energy and stress. If we do not have enough cortisol, we are going to use adrenalin, an emergency hormone that has a lightning bolt effect. For many years, cortisol has had a bad name because scientists have pointed out that under stress, cortisol goes up and that is true. If cortisol ranges from 6 to 25 and you are in a car wreck, it will jump to 300; however, what if you had a car wreck every day? The first week it might go to 300, the next week it would go to 200, and the week after that 100; eventually, you would end up where my patients are whose bodies think they are going through car wrecks every two hours. The body will not be able to respond. Personally, my cortisol is never higher than 5 on a normal range of 6 to 25. When we measure cortisol, we find almost all my patients are in the lower range of normal or below normal. So that while it is true that cortisol is a stress hormone and it is bad in that it goes up under stressful situations, we *need* cortisol to get through our daily lives without stress. However, if our daily lives are filled with too much stress or stress levels that are too high, our body will not make more cortisol; the body will exhaust its ability to make cortisol and it will start *misusing* adrenalin as a replacement. This is what most of us see happening after college. During college, even though we ran ourselves ragged, had way too much activity, and kept extremely long hours, we still had enough cortisol (all of our hormone levels were higher) so that we could rest and recover during the night. However, as we get older, we run out of cortisol more and more and now have to run more and more on adrenalin.

Cortisol usually comes out in most people in a burst in the morning; we have our best energy first thing in the morning when we wake up and it goes down during the day. All humans have what are called *circadian rhythms*, physiological and behavioral rhythms controlled by our hormones. Almost all humans have a *circadian dip* in cortisol, a daily dip that occurs between and 2:00 and 6:00 in the afternoon. I call this "sleepy time." I start yawning automatically about 3:00 o'clock, and I am going to feel a little sleepy until about 6:00 p.m. Then, some more cortisol kicks in IF I can get through that period, and I will feel pretty good. I will have a little resurgence of energy and I will feel good until I run out of cortisol. As we get older, we notice how cortisol starts occurring earlier and earlier, so that now I find it very hard to stay awake past 10 o'clock at night. I start getting sleepy now at about 8 o'clock, so I settle down and start reading about 8:30, knowing I will be asleep by 9:30 to 10:00. While I will wake up in the middle of the night, I will force myself to go back to sleep and sleep lightly until it is time to get up between 4:00 and 5:00. Everybody notices this change in their cortisol level as they get older . . . everybody. Once in a great while, I will run into somebody who has high levels of cortisol all day and into the night. But, they do *not* have fibromyalgia and they do *not* have any of these other problems. There are some people in this world who have good hormones until the day they die. I do not see these folks as patients. They do not come to my office. Why would someone who feels "great" go see any doctor? The patients I see do have a hormone imbalance. The patients I see have severe symptoms. AND, whatever symptoms we have are made worse by adrenalin.

As you might expect, many night shift workers' immune systems are messed up. There were many more accidents with night fliers in the war, many more, and much higher incidents of injuries, accidents, and miscalculations. You are going against Nature if you try to get somebody to sleep by day and work by night, and you are going to have some problems. While there may be a few people that are on that cycle and do well with it, most will find it stressful. We have been discussing toward the end of this last section how pain caused by adrenalin leads to a number of problems including restless sleep. Naturally, this can only lead to overwhelming tiredness and profound fatigue. We will now discuss the fourth of our five basic symptoms that are encountered most often in hormone imbalance and treatment.

Fatigue

"Doctor, I just don't have any energy. I get up and I start moving around and within five minutes, I feel like I have to go back to bed. Anything I do just leaves me completely and utterly exhausted. Whenever I get up and try to do something, I am just floored. If I walk across the room, I feel like I'm going to fall over and collapse." This is a common complaint of many of my patients.

I see some cases of fatigue that are so severe that the patients feel like they cannot move at all. In my view, a hormone imbalance can lead to an excessive use of adrenalin, which will lead to the most profound fatigue that a patient can imagine or experience. The feeling of fatigue is genuine; they have absolutely no energy. Not only have they run out of cortisol, which we have discussed above, but now they are running out of adrenalin as well. This is the classic *chronic fatigue syndrome* patient who simply cannot move at all. Fortunately, there are some solutions to this. These patients are usually low in all their hormones, even adrenalin. These are the patients who will lie in bed for two days and get a little bit of energy, so they get up and try to use that little surge of energy to catch up on all the things they need to do. They try to catch up on two days' worth of work in two hours while they have this little surge of energy. This, of course, inevitably leads to the next collapse two hours later, and down they go again. Now they are down and out for another 24-48 hours; then, they get a few hours of energy and they repeat the same process. Once again, God teaches them that they have chronic fatigue syndrome and they end up in bed unable to move.

I try to explain to these people that I have to get them moving. They absolutely have to move. If patients cannot move, I cannot help them. I do not care if they have no legs, I want them to lie in bed and use rubber bands or lift soup cans short of the point where they feel exhaustion. The problem is that, knowing they only have a brief period when they are going to have energy, they try to cram as much into it as they can. They do this because they realize they are going to be knocked back down. I suggest to them that this is a *huge* mistake, and that I need them to know where that cutoff point is and always stay short of it. I want them to do movement just short of the point where they find themselves exhausted. For somebody who cannot walk across the room, that might be sitting up every hour for 30 seconds and then the next day will try sitting up every hour for 40 seconds, and so forth.

I want them to walk slowly for one hour before they go to bed to get rid of this adrenalin, so that they will rest more. They explain carefully to me that I simply do not understand. They are too tired to walk. Naturally, I have to spend a lot of time helping people understand that even though they have profound fatigue, they are not really *tired*; they just *seem* tired because of adrenalin. After all, if we were *really* tired, rest would fix this, and it does not. If one of these people were to get Grandma to take care of the babies and tell the husband that they were going to be busy for 48 hours, then go to sleep on Friday night and not get up until Monday morning, they would feel worse. The longer we lie down, the worse we feel, unless we really need rest. If we really need rest, then we will wake up refreshed after an extended period of sleep. But my experience and that of most of my patients is that the longer they lie down, the *worse* they feel.

They are going to come home and lie down at night because they *feel* tired. My point would be this: do not go to bed until you are ready to go to sleep. If you lie down when you come home at night, say 8:00 o'clock at night, as you lie back, your brain will begin to swell even more and it will knock you out – not because you are tired, but because of the effect of gravity on your head. If I come home in the evening and sit down to watch the evening news, I will fall asleep and I will not wake up for an hour or two. I will have missed the news because I would promptly fall asleep, and that is because I am sitting still and my brain swells.

My classic example is in my own case: my wife used to say of me that I ran 12 miles, four times a year. By that, she meant I would go out and run so fast I would pull a tendon and the ligaments would be stressed. I would lie down and heal for three months, and then I would get up and try the 12 miles again. Well, it does not take many years of that cycle before one realizes that three miles every day at a much slower pace might allow me to accomplish a whole lot more miles per year than my insane 12-mile runs. I really have a hard time getting patients to slow down enough and diminish the intensity to the point where they do not hurt themselves. Even Runner's World talks about runners who have reached the point where they have chronic fatigue syndrome, they simply cannot run anymore, and the same solutions are being proposed for them. Even though you used to be a marathon runner, maybe you are going to have to start shuffling slowly with a slow walk to restore your muscle strength and your energy while we balance your hormones so that you can do something without using adrenalin.

➢ SLOWER CAN BE BETTER

When I was in grade school, the nuns used to say to us that we should try to do God's will. I held my hand up and asked, "How do I know what God's will is?" The nun responded, "You can only tell the next day. The next day, if the result of what you did was good, then you probably did God's will; if the result was bad, you didn't." This is the rule I want you to apply to movement and exercise. If you feel better afterward, you did the right amount. If you feel worse, you messed up. I do not care how little or how mild it was, if you feel worse, you did too much. The patients say, "But I used to run marathons," and I say, "Well, you used to be a 12-year-old sixth grader too, but you are not anymore." With this hormone imbalance, the only way we will ever get it anywhere back close to normal is we have to get them out of the habit of using adrenalin. In order to do that, they are going to have to do incredibly slow, mild movement. Suppose somebody is used to walking briskly three miles a day and then feeling completely wiped out for 48 hours. What if we cut that to one mile at a slow pace and found they were *not* wiped out afterward? What if they did it for a week while I put the hormones back in balance? Then the next week, they might do one and a half miles at the same slow pace. With this kind of increase, within a month they are doing three or four miles at a fairly reasonable pace, and *feel good every time.* We must get below the "crash and burn" level every time. However, if every time they go out, they completely exhaust themselves using adrenalin, they will never make progress.

Consequently, most of them tell me, "I can't exercise; it kills me." I say, "Well you cannot exercise like you were; but what if we tried something a little slower, less intense?" This works for a while and then we run into the ever constant problem of all humans; as soon as they get better, they declare themselves well and go right back to their old bad habits. Then, in one or two weeks, they drift back into the same patterns that led to the problems in the first place. It *always* happens, so we warn everybody, "You are going to take this all back in a month and you are going to be right back where you started. Then, I hope you will go back to your notes and start over and restrict your foods and do the low-intensity, *boring* exercise. Eventually, we hope you will learn what you are capable of doing and learn your limitations." This is very difficult for people, particularly those who are "recovering" athletes, to realize that this is now an entirely different world than the one of their athletic youth. They have to find some different levels that they can accomplish without crashing so that they can build themselves up. They have the athletic ambitions of a teenage athlete, but they have the hormone levels of a really old person. Well, the only way you can bridge that gap is with adrenalin. So, I want them to reduce the intensity of their exercise, of all their movement, of all their activities, down to the level of their hormones, which is very low intensity indeed. If you used to be a sprinter, now I want you to be a crawler until you can learn to walk, then learn to jog, then learn to run, and eventually sprint again. If I can reduce the intensity of their exercise down to the level of their hormones and then bring the exercise intensity and the hormones up together, we will be successful. If they get the bit in their teeth and take off, they are going to crash and burn.

No one understands that *hormones run the body*, not even the doctors. If they do not know it, they are not informing the patients. Athletes think they have to work through the pain (e.g., "no pain, no gain"), but that is so wrong. We are talking about movement, not exercise; exercise is a bad word and has a bad connotation. I do an enormous amount of really vigorous exercise, but I have to counter it with the low-intensity movement before bed. We will get these folks back up there where they can do almost anything. They are capable of marathons, kickboxing, whatever it might be; but we have to bring their hormones and their movement up together. They cannot go from here to there in a flash. Everybody is impatient; they want to be right where they used to be, right now. It just doesn't work that way.

➢ IS IT REALLY "FATIGUE"?

Let me tell you something else about fatigue. The important thing, I think, for a patient to know and remember about fatigue is that it is often not real. They feel fatigued, but they are not. If it were really fatigue, sleep would make it better and in these cases, it does not make it better. We use the example of PMS. Many women experience PMS, which is an altered state. I remind the women, "Remember 30 years ago when you were first married and had some severe cramping and mood alteration with PMS? Once in awhile you would wake up, look over at your husband, and think, 'I'm going to kill him.' But then, you would stop yourself and say, 'No, I'm not; it's just my hormones. I'm not going to kill him. He doesn't deserve to die . . . yet.'" So, you would forgo that pleasure for the time being anyway.

That is the way I want you to look at fatigue; it may be a trick, it may just be the feeling you have when you are operating on adrenalin. He did not really need to die and you do not *really* need to feel fatigued. It is not real. You will feel just as tired if you get up and start walking. If you do start walking, slowly you will feel a great deal better because you will have had some movement. However, if you believe this false signal of fatigue, you are going to lie down, your brain is going to swell some more, and tomorrow you are going to feel even worse. If, on the other hand, you *dis*believe the signal of fatigue and you believe me that it is just a trick your brain is playing on you, then you are going to be able to override that feeling of fatigue. You are going to get up and start walking and we all know you will feel better if you can start moving . . . moving so slowly you don't cause worse exhaustion. You know that, I know that, every patient has always told me that; but they are not going to walk because they are too tired. However, what if you are not really tired? What if it is a trick? If you complain to your doctor, what is he going to give you? An antidepressant. He is going to shut you up. If you take enough antidepressant, you indeed will not feel so tired . . . you will not feel *anything*.

So, here you are struggling to feel more and more alert, which means more adrenalin, more fat, less sex drive, and an altered state. If you are on antidepressants, who are you? I mean, if you complain to the doctor, you know what he is going to do: double the dose. If you continue to complain, he will add a second antidepressant until he shuts you up. In medical school, we laughingly refer to antidepressants as *chemical restraints*; it shuts the patient up. Also, I promise you, if those patients continue complaining, somebody will eventually operate on them. They will do an "exploratory" surgery in your belly, your shoulder, or wherever you hurt. They are going to look in there and see if they can find out what is causing all these problems. Even though "the problem" moves from your left shoulder to your right, from day to day, somebody will offer to operate.

Short-term Memory Loss

Another common symptom I see in patients who come to my office is loss of short-term memory. Loss of short-term memory seems to be more common in females, or perhaps they are more willing to admit it than males. I personally experienced this when I was about 32 years old as a surgery resident. The first time I really got sick that I can recall with allergy problems, I had been sick in bed for a week. I decided that if I was going to be recovering and sick, I ought to try and do some studying. So, I got my notes out and began to read them. I realized that I could not remember anything that I had just read. The print was flying by, and I did not have diminished short-term memory, I had *no* short-term memory. I could not remember a single line that I had read, which was a big shock for me because I was used to a nearly photographic memory.

I hear this a great deal from women, and the complaints are increasingly common as they get older. Almost all my patients over 60 are complaining to me about their short-term memory loss. They want to know if the treatment for weight problems, pain problems, fibromyalgia, diminished sex drive, and all the other things that we deal with will improve their short-term memory as well. I think it is important to realize that they have not *lost* their minds or their memories, they have just *misplaced* them. They are denied the use of them for some period of time, particularly when they are under stress, when they are tired, when they run out of energy, or when they are allergic. If there is something enormously stressful going on, we may not remember where we left our car, and this can happen with increasing frequency as we get older. We run more and more on adrenalin, which really short-circuits all of our smooth running equipment, so that if we were sitting in a completely quiet environment and were completely rested, we might well have a highly refined short-term memory. But if somebody yelled "Fire!" and we heard sirens and somebody came pounding on the front door, I am fairly confident that short-term memory would disappear instantly because of the incredible surge of electrical activity that accompanies adrenalin. Well, most of my patients are in a highly adrenalized state most of the time, so it is an absolute wonder that we function as well as we do. I have 34 women employed in my office. They have to remind me what to do every hour of every day. Even at that, I have stick-it notes posted all over my car, my mirror, and in my billfold. It is harder and harder to keep track of all the things of which we would like to keep track. Yes, it is true that things get more complex and we have more things to track, but I did not have nearly this much trouble remembering things when I was 20.

➢ FATIGUE AND FOOD

Like all of the other problems we have discussed in this section, the problem with short-term memory is an excess of adrenalin and a lack of restful, relaxing movement. Long . . . slow . . . distance will help this. Likewise, a modified diet would contribute to a smooth functioning memory. Most of my patients find foods and drinks that make them feel better, more alert, or make them feel more relaxed or sleepy. I think I can "drug" myself with everything I need coming from the grocery store. If a heroin addict wakes up in the morning feeling terrible and is having a really bad day, he needs some of his drug. If an alcoholic wakes up and feels like that, he does not need heroin, he needs a drink. If I wake up feeling like that, my head is fuzzy, I am allergic to something in the air, and I just feel like I cannot function. Three drugs will wake me up and make me feel much better:

strong coffee, dark chocolate, or real Coca-Cola. Any one of those things will wake me up very quickly and effectively. On the other hand, if I want to go to sleep at night and I am really desperate, I can eat a big plate of pasta, or a pizza, or some Baskin-Robbins Rocky Road ice cream, and you could not wake me with a gun. Within 15 minutes, I will be unconscious.

We have learned that certain things make us feel better and certain things make us feel more relaxed or sleepy; these are dangerous foods and are having a drugging effect upon us. Ordinary people go through the store and they do not pass through sections where foods call out to them. When I pass through the bread section, little voices call out and say, "Buy me; eat me." I know people who do not experience that. If I go to a French Restaurant and start on the bread, I do not need a menu, I just need another basket of bread and more butter, and I am not even going to remember whom I am there with because my head will get so foggy so fast. I have many patients who experience this, and yet we are in the habit of eating certain foods, even those we consider to be healthy, organic foods (i.e., organic ice cream or organic chocolate). Nevertheless, if we react to these foods, then they are going to have a drug effect on us and they will affect our energy levels and our short-term memory. I do not think there is a mother that I have ever encountered that did not realize that her children were little food addicts. If she has three children, she has to get three kinds of cereal, three kinds of fruit juice, and three kinds of vegetables, because everybody has foods that affect them differently. Certainly, there are those of us who have these hormone imbalances and food allergies. I am sure there are ordinary people who go to the store or go to the restaurant, order moderate portions, and do not have any further problem. If I start on chocolate, it is not a question of how much chocolate can I eat; the question is how much have you got? So, those of us who have food allergies, memory issues, energy issues, fatigue issues, and pain issues are affected by the "drugs" we put in our bodies.

So, why does this occur? Memory is dramatically affected by swelling. I think the two hemispheres of the brain operate interdependently and that there is a synchronous hum of electrical activity between the two sides of the brain. When the two sides swell, they swell differently, so there is a disconnect. Anything that makes the brain swell will cause an interruption of the signals, and that is when the memory goes. Airborne allergy makes the ear tubes and the nasal sinus passages swell; this backs up pressure in the brain, the brain disconnects, and then there is "nobody home." If we have swelling of the brain – if the patients are experiencing PMS swelling or drink some beer and feel pressure and swelling in the front of their heads – they are not going to remember much. Memory is affected by swelling in the front part of the brain and anything that causes that swelling will cause an impairment of memory. Some of the things that cause swelling are airborne allergies, hormone allergies, fatigue, stress, foods, drinks, and drugs. The solution to the swelling is to move more fluid *through* the brain. If we want to feel more alert, all we have to do is get up and start walking around at a moderate pace. This will clear the congestion out of the front part of the brain, and we will feel more alert. Most people who do vigorous exercise comment on the fact of how bright the lights seem when they finish, how clear their thinking is, and how crisp the smells are. We feel terribly alert when we have had some vigorous activity. On the other hand, in order to prevent adrenalin surges, I suggest activity, but not that vigorous. When someone feels like their mental capacity is diminishing late in the afternoon, instead of drinking a cup of coffee or a Coca-Cola and trying harder, I would like them to get up and walk around for five minutes and drink a glass of water.

➢ FATIGUE AND REST

The United States Government, in its infinite wisdom, blows a whistle every hour and all the troops in training sit down for 10 minutes. The government does not do this out of any great sense of sympathy or generosity. They do it because they know that troops will get more done at the end of each day if they *force* them to take breaks . . . to rest. My patients do not do that. Many of my patients are in executive positions and all the professional people I see get themselves a little behind, and they start feeling a little memory loss, or loss of energy, and they *redouble* their efforts. They ramp up the intensity of whatever they are doing. They work harder and longer and, of course, they see diminishing returns. So I try and convince them that if they would work a little less hard and spend 10 minutes out of each hour walking around and clearing their head and getting this congestion out of their brain, they would function much better. Furthermore, if they would leave work two hours early instead of staying at work two hours later, go home, and walk slowly for an hour, they would wake up so much more refreshed and so much more alert the next day that they would get more work done than if they had stayed late.

The British Army discovered this in the 18th Century. A statistician went out with the troops, and on an experiment, he had the marching troops sit down for 10 minutes each hour. Lo, and behold, their conclusion at the end of a yearlong study was that the troops who took the breaks covered more miles by the end of each day. Well, the British Army was smart enough to use that information. To this day, many organizations, corporations in Japan, the British Army, and the American Army enforce rest periods so they will get more efficiency. We, as individuals, do not do that. All the people I see seem to be individual gladiators, gunfighters, and self-made wrecks. When we get behind, we just redouble our efforts. We work harder, even though the results are worse. I spend great amounts of time trying to get people not necessarily to slow down but to work in a more focused fashion. If you cannot think straight, don't try to turn up the voltage; just stop and step back, walk around for a few minutes, let your head clear, and then go back to work.

In summary, short-term memory is greatly affected by swelling in the brain. Swelling is addressed by movement, by correct diet, and by reducing stress. If you do not know you are under stress then there is no way you are going to be able to combat it. As we noted above, we will frequently recommend a pulse meter. The people around you know when you are under stress, but it is just a fact of life that we frequently do not. We do not know until it is full-blown, the chest gets tight, the heart races, the throat gets tight, and we cannot remember where we left the get-away car. Short term memory loss can be improved by exercise, diet, and hormones, and all these things can be addressed quite easily. Someone asks, "So, you would treat the short-term memory loss the same way you would treat these other things, by balancing the hormones and changing the lifestyle?" The answer is a resounding "Yes." If hormones are out of balance, you are going to run on adrenalin. Adrenalin is the key factor here: it causes many of our problems and many things can help reduce its over-use.

Chapter 3

Personal Stories

This chapter contains several examples of individuals who have had typical problems, who came to the Roby Institute in Austin, and who now live normal and productive lives. Not only are these stories real, they are only samples of thousands that we could tell. Plainly and simply, we are helping people reclaim their lives through the methods we employ in treating the causes of their pain when others have refused to consider these causes as possibilities for what is ailing these folks. We hope by presenting these "testimonials" that you can find yourself in some of these stories. We have tried to select those that are representative of the types of problems we see on a day-to-day basis in the office. Keep one thing in mind: the people who I see in my office are intense, focused, very busy, and productive people. Even people with diminished mental capacities I see, we find are very intense individuals. They are often highly adrenalized. They always have projects going, usually way too many, and these complexities in their lives either trigger or magnify the physical problems they encounter. I have alluded to a period of time in my life that prompted me to begin this journey of discovery that I have traveled for the past 30 years. I will begin with my own story and then we'll move to the others.

Dr. Roby – Food Allergy

I first became acquainted with the things we have been discussing up to this point in the book when it happened to me. I have always been a pretty healthy fellow and had not had any kind of symptoms all through my days in college. I do not ever remember being sick in any way. Even as a kid I never needed much sleep and got by on four to five hours of sleep each night, waking up perfectly refreshed every morning. I had a very clear memory and was a pretty good student. By 23, I was licensed to practice law in Texas. After a few years as a lawyer, however, I decided I wanted to become a physician; I wanted to be a transplant surgeon. In order to get into medical school, I had to do a lot of pre-med work and graduate work, and my graduate advisor suggested that in graduate school I study something that would help me to become a better transplant surgeon. I decided to study immunology for my Ph.D. work; I completed my Ph.D. prelims and was fairly well along in my research when I began medical school.

It was in medical school that I had the worst academic experience in my life. I found that we were memorizing all our material. There was no time for discussion and no time for questions. We were fully occupied memorizing the material. Medical doctors are the best prepared people on earth to treat the thousands of diseases that we memorized. We memorized thousands of diseases and thousands of drugs, and the finals were about connecting the dots. Occasionally when drugs did not work, there would be surgical solutions to some of the medical problems. I made it through but it was not terribly interesting. I memorized it because I was still determined to become a transplant surgeon, and you had to get through medical school to do that.

I started my internship in 1973, and within a couple of months, I became terribly ill. I had contracted some type of flu and I was confined to bed. In cardiovascular surgery rotations in those days, interns were expected to sleep about four hours every other night and all the rest of the time we stayed at work. I could do that and many young men did, but it is very hard on your system. With the flu, I was flat on my back for a week. As I slowly recovered from the nausea, vomiting, and fever, I was still unable to get up. I was still devastatingly tired, so I decided I would spend my time studying my notes; studying is what I did best. I began to read my notes and in no time at all I began to realize I could not understand what I was reading. I saw the words floating by in front of my face, but they did not mean anything to me. As you might guess, I got quite alarmed and I tried to study harder. I drank a couple cups of coffee, got a yellow highlighter, and I tried to really focus. It was alarming to me that I could not remember what I was reading. I worked for a few minutes and I looked up and realized I had just colored an entire page yellow . . . and I had no idea what it said.

Now I was really in a panic. I called the doctor who was managing my case and told him I thought I had a brain tumor. I wanted it fixed immediately because there was something seriously wrong with my brain. I was put in the hospital and I was kept in there for six days while every test known to man was run on me. They tested everything they could think of. After several days of tests, a little group of doctors came in with big smiles on their faces, announcing to me that I was "just fine" and that there was nothing wrong with me. As you might imagine, I was a little taken aback, because I still could not get out of bed; 18 hours of sleep was not enough, and when I got up, I could barely walk. I said, "It seems damn strange that I could be 'just fine' and still feel so terrible." The head doctor said, "Well, we know you feel bad, but these tests clearly indicate that there is nothing wrong with you." He had some tests indicating that not only were all my laboratory studies and all the diagnostic studies normal, they were high normal, so he was perfectly confident in explaining to me that there was absolutely nothing wrong with me. I asked him, "How do you explain the fact that I can't get out of bed." He said, "That's easy. We think it is caused by stress." I responded, "Let me explain something to you: I was a trial lawyer for five years; that was stress . . . this isn't." He said, "Well, if it's not stress, we are forced to conclude . . . it must be emotional." I said, "Well, that's just the damndest thing I ever heard. How is that conceivably possible?" He said, "Well, that's the only choice we have left. Would you consider seeing a psychiatrist?" I said, "Sure, I would see an exorcist if it would fix it!"

So, now I am lined up to see a psychiatrist. I am to visit with him for an hour every day; I have no other duties. At the first visit, we sat there and visited for about 15 minutes, he leaned back in his chair, smiled, and said, "Son, you seem depressed, so I'm going to put you on an antidepressant." I said, "Well, hell yes, I'm depressed. I can't do my job. But nobody got divorced. Nobody died. There is no reason for me to be depressed, except that I don't feel good and I am too tired to get out of bed." He said, "Well, I think we will put you on antidepressants." I said, "No, we are not going to do that. I have seen people on antidepressants and you just water them once a week. That will end my career for sure." He said, "Well, I think you need to be on antidepressants." We left it at that. Then, we began to discuss whether or not my mother had abused me when I was a child. This whole line of questioning was making me furious.

I have 30 days to get it together or get out. But there is no way I can sit around for 30 days and simply visit with this guy for an hour a day. I was really casting about for a project that would occupy my time, so I decided I would put myself in perfect physical condition. In the four years of my medical school experience, I had stopped all my running, I ate trash, and I did nothing but study, so I had gained 50 pounds. I thought, "I will use these 30 days to lose 30 pounds." I grew up in Catholic schools; in a Catholic school whenever you want to see God or lose weight, you fasted (ate no food). I would start with a seven-day fast, start walking and jogging two hours a day, and then continue to diet after the initial seven-day fast. I began this and at the end of four days, *all my symptoms were gone*. My head was clear as a bell, I was sleeping four and a half to five hours a night, my memory was back, and I felt like a million dollars. I discussed this with the psychiatrist and he found it so fascinating that he began to jog with me in the morning. He was a little cloudy-headed (I already knew this) and he thought it might help him. By the end of 10 days, I was treating my shrink, his wife, and his two teenage children. All of us had modified what we were eating, we were running, and everybody was feeling better and better.

I went back and explained to my doctor that I was suffering from food allergy. He snickered and said, "Well son, you know there is no such thing as food allergy, but I'm happy that psychotherapy is working effectively for you." I was mystified that nobody seemed to understand what was going on. Consequently, I decided that I would prove that he was wrong. Now, one of the things I do best in this life is libraries. So, I went and plopped myself in the medical school library and began to investigate the area of food allergy. Lo, and behold, at the end of two days, I had to come to the same conclusion that he had: there was no such thing as food allergy – at least not in medical literature. There were a few isolated examples of somebody who ate a peanut and died on the spot, but other than these bizarre cases or anaphylactic reactions to a few foods and a small number of patients, there was no such thing as food allergy. Yet, it was terribly clear to me that if I ate very carefully during the week or fasted and then went to Shakey's Pizza Parlor on Friday night, drank a pitcher of beer, and had a pizza, you might as well call an ambulance to get me home because I become unconscious when I eat certain foods. Well, I had this startling revelation that medicine has a huge blind spot in its body of knowledge. Apparently, we have the finest doctors on earth for detecting and treating a very large number of well-defined diseases that they study, but then a peculiar thing happens: If you are not in that book of disorders, then you do not exist. They take the strange point of view that if they cannot *find* it, you do not *have* it. This revelation was so clear to me. It was very obvious from my own experience in my own case (and that of the psychiatrist, his family, and several other people I was talking to) that many, many people suffer from disorders that medicine doesn't know anything about. This is frustrating for the doctors and devastating for the patients.

MacKenzie – Interstitial Cystitis Case No. 1

Four years ago when I was 17, I began suffering from Urinary Tract Infections (UTI's) on a regular basis along with pain in my lower abdomen. My family doctor attributed the pain to the UTI's. I was treated with Pyridium and Macrodantin since I was allergic to Cipro. After two months of not finding relief and symptoms that became worse, I began my long journey on eventually being diagnosed with Interstitial Cystitis (IC). I went from general practitioners, to urologists, to gynecologists, to iridologists, and even to kinesiologists, searching for a diagnosis and cure to my pain. I was diagnosed with anything from kidney stones, to endometriosis, to ovarian cysts, and then finally with IC. IC is a constant hemorrhaging of the bladder because there isn't a bladder lining. This not only causes mild to severe pain on a regular basis, but also frequent and urgent impulses to urinate, pain on urination, lower back pain, and loss of appetite because food would usually lead to pain. Aside from the traditional IC pain that I was having, I would monthly (following the exact cycle of my period) have severe stabbing pains in my lower abdomen that would result in an emergency room hospital visit. Each visit would result in CT Scans, MRIs, crazy looks from the ER doctors, and a dose of Demerol or morphine. The ER doctors' only explanation was an ovarian cyst that was rupturing. However, that was their *best guess* as none of the tests were definitive.

On a daily basis, my pain levels would range (on a scale of 1–10 where 10 is maximum pain) from a 4 to 6 (on a good day) and an 8 to 9 when the "ovarian cyst" would rupture. My "best friend" was my pain medication and I hated relying on that to just get through the day. Over the course of the four years, I had three surgeries and multiple treatments that were unsuccessful in diagnosing me and treating my pain. I finally ended up at Vanderbilt Hospital where I was diagnosed with IC. I then went through the conventional route of treatments. The first thing that I tried to do was to change my diet. The diet was called the "IC Diet." I was to abstain from eating anything salty, spicy, acidic, or too sweet. Needless to say, this was not an easy regimen for a college student. After trying the IC Diet and having little success, I then moved on to the drugs Elmiron and Elavil, the medicinal combination that is supposed to help heal the bladder lining and ease pain. This medication resulted in slight hallucinations from the Elavil and loss of hair from the Elmiron, yet little, if any, relief or cure. My next course of action was to endure the nine-week bladder instillation treatments; these instillations were administered at the doctor's office through a small catheter. What was instilled was a mixture of bicarbonate, Lidocaine, and Marcaine. This was supposed to numb the bladder so that pain wouldn't be felt, to slough off the remaining dead lining, and to build a new bladder lining. I did not have luck with these instillations and continued to suffer with a disease that apparently had no known cause and no known cure.

Nothing was giving me any hope. I wasn't getting any better, and at times, I felt I was getting worse. I was trying to go to school and work but was barely able to keep the schedule I had. I would get out of bed to just do what I absolutely had to do, then I was back at home in bed. I was miserable. I was watching my life pass me by, coming to grips with the fact that I was never going to be normal.

My parents were distraught. We had exhausted all of our options, except for placing a TENS Unit (a battery-operated device that sends electrical impulses to parts of the body to block pain) into my body or *surgically removing my bladder*. Neither of these solutions was particularly appealing, understandably, so my family and I were slowly starting to feel that this was a battle I was never going to win. In desperate attempts to learn more about this disease and how to find relief, my mother bought numerous books on Interstitial Cystitis. In one of the books, Mom found an author who suggested that IC might be related to *hormones* and hormonal imbalances. In her desperation to find some relief for me, she decided to search online about *hormone imbalances*. She finally came to the site of the Roby Institute at http://www.robyinstitute.com. As she read through the site, she was given some serious hope. She made a call to his office and spoke with Dr. Roby directly. At a total loss for how to help her daughter, she was in tears on the phone with him. Dr. Roby quickly calmed her and explained his practices to her. He said that he was confident that he could help with my problems and I would feel improvement after one visit to his office. This sounded way too good to be true. It sounded ridiculous and fraudulent, but we were willing to try anything that offered us any vestige of hope. We had been through such a long, depressing journey just to get to a diagnosis, to say nothing of the four solid years of suffering. At this point, no matter what was offered to us as an alternative to surgical bladder removal, we were willing to try it.

We made an appointment for January 3, 2006. Since that day, I have never felt better. Leaving his office that day, I *was* absolutely pain free! I wish that I could put into words the feelings and emotions that came over me that day as I sat in his office and tried different hormones hoping to find the one that "worked" for me. Dr. Roby placed a few drops of each hormone under my tongue. After a few tests, he found the hormone causing the pain. Once we found that one hormone that was causing the problem, my pain was gone. I sat in his office and cried, telling my mom over and over again, "I have no pain. My pain is gone." Needless to say, my mom was crying, too.

My pain was being caused by an allergic reaction to one of my own hormones. I also was overusing my adrenal gland, so any exertion of energy at all would leave me extremely tired and in pain. Dr. Roby was able to correct this by evaluating my blood work and trying different hormone supplements on me. He placed a few drops of these different hormones underneath my tongue, and I would immediately notice a change in the way I felt – either better or worse. Once we realized exactly which hormone my body was reacting to, I noticed an immediate reduction in my pain. Within seconds, I was pain free. Dr. Roby placed me on a regimen for balancing my hormones and also placed me on an eating program that would help control any potential "flares," as well as make me feel better overall. He also gave me

Buffered C, a powder to mix in with a drink, to help calm any flare that couldn't be blocked by a hormone.

Since that day, there have been days when I have had pain. Those pains were easily traceable to the fact that I had overworked or overstressed myself, allowing my hormones to become unbalanced. Even this pain, however, is nowhere near what I was feeling prior to seeing Dr. Roby. I take my hormones and allergens regularly, which takes care of my pain. When I have "overdone it" in one way or another and am having problems finding the right combinations of hormones, I call Dr. Roby and he walks me through steps to find the right levels that I need. I also carefully monitor my diet and stress levels to make sure that I do not unintentionally cause myself pain. I am careful to eat foods that do not contain a high amount of sugar and I stay away from most acidic foods (tomatoes, citrus fruits, fruit juices, etc.). I have begun to wear a pulse meter to measure my heart rate. I have an alarm on the pulse meter to let me know when my heart rate gets above a certain level so that I can take the time to lower my heart rate, and in turn, lower my adrenalin flow. This also helps to make sure that I do not go into a "flare" with pain because I have overworked myself.

This has been such an easy and simple solution to such a huge and unmanageable problem that consumed my life for so long. On my four–year journey with IC, I saw eight doctors and went through three surgeries before finding the final solution with Dr. Roby. Without him and his knowledge and understanding of the adrenal gland and the hormone, I would still be practically homebound or worse. Because of him, I am now "normal." I have been able to continue my life in the way that I always hoped that I would. Because we caught my situation at such a young age, it is likely that my hormones will eventually kick in and take over; that seems to be happening as I now take them only when I have overdone something to get me out of balance. I have been able to marry, have a full-time job, exercise on a regular basis, and enjoy my days because I feel great. Without Dr. Roby, I fear that I would have been a physical and emotional wreck, never being able to live the life I am currently living. I owe the fact that I now have a normal life and future to Dr. Roby and all he has done for me. He has given so much back to me; the least that I can do is let others know about him through offering my story here and about the great things that he has done for me.

Sarah – Recovery from Interstitial Cystitis (London, UK) Case No. 2

Interstitial Cystitis (IC) is a painful and debilitating bladder condition that wreaks havoc in the lives of women and men (but mainly women) in the US, as well as abroad. It is a condition with which I am, sadly, very familiar as I have lived with it for the past four years. I am now, however, well on the road to recovery and would like to share my story with you in the hope that it inspires and encourages those who are living with this condition.

Through my research into IC, I have learned that IC pain may be equivalent to end stage cancer pain. The quality of life of IC patients may be worse than that of a kidney dialysis patient. IC can irreparably damage the social life, sex life, career, and relationships of those who suffer with it. During my four years with IC, every day there was some sort and level of pain: burning pain, stinging pain, aching pain, cutting pain, pinching pain, and stabbing pain. Some days, it was bearable; others, it was not. Sometimes I was still able focus on other things in my life; at other times, I was completely distracted by the pain. Physical pain went hand in hand with emotional suffering: anger, hurt, frustration, disappointment, bewilderment, confusion, irritability, despondence, and devastation.

I have spent days and days researching this condition and hour upon hour with different healthcare professionals: consultants, GPs, nurses, and alternative health practitioners. Most of them have tried their best to help me. Many have made promises, which did not materialize. Some of them have been very compassionate. But throughout, the pain remained.

At the beginning of my journey with IC, I asked my healthcare providers whether it was possible that my pain was connected to my hormones. Throughout my teens and early 20s, I suffered with an eating disorder. I lost my periods on many occasions. Usually they came back, but for years on end, I would not have a period. I was in my early 20s when my IC symptoms developed. It seemed logical, therefore, to me that my hormones may be involved. The doctors I suggested this to belittled my ideas. They all but laughed at me. I have no medical training and have been brought up to trust doctors. Therefore, I believed them when they told me I was wrong.

Years later, I came back to my hormone theory as nothing else was working and I was at the end of my rope. I was crying every day, couldn't work because of the pain, and was shouting at everyone who loved me because I could not cope anymore. One day as I searched the Web through tears, I came across Dr Roby's Web site. I was given some major hope for the first time in three years. The information on the Web site seemed to be telling me that I was right: addressing my hormones may be the key to my recovery. At the time, I did not live near Dr. Roby, so I began to communicate with him by email and phone. I found him to be extremely helpful, caring, and knowledgeable. He explained how hormone imbalance and allergy could lead to a range of distressing symptoms, including bladder pain. He gave me a recovery plan that included hormone balancing, stress reduction, and improvements to my diet. On his advice, I arranged to have my hormone levels tested and shared the results with Dr. Roby. The results showed that my estrogen levels were very low – similar to those of an 80-year-old woman. No wonder I was feeling rough!

I worked with Dr. Roby on a long distance basis at first. I was under the care of a doctor in London, who subscribed to the hormone-IC theory. He prescribed bioidentical hormones to increase my estrogen levels to within normal limits. Within two weeks, my symptoms had reduced. I couldn't believe it! After three years of pain and so many different treatments, it took just two weeks to feel a difference.

Later on, we moved to the United States so I could be closer to Dr. Roby. I was able to meet Dr. Roby in person due to our fortuitous move to Texas. He was able to treat me in person and add the progesterone drops to my treatment program in order to address my progesterone sensitivity, and I have continued to get better and better.

Today, my pain levels are way down and I live a normal life. I can go for whole days without even thinking about my bladder, which is miraculous for me. I believe I will continue to improve to the point when IC is a distant memory for me. I do not like to use the word "cured" as I do not want to jinx myself and my health is an ongoing project for me. However, I am keen to share my story with others in the hope that it can help people in similar situations. If you are living with the horrific and relentless pain of IC, I would urge you to consider that hormones may be involved in your case and discuss this with Dr. Roby.

Becky – Chronic Pain

Three years ago, I was 22 years old, finishing my last semester of college, and planning a wedding. In my last couple of years of college, I had begun to suffer from headaches and neck pain on a regular basis (my pain level was probably about a 2 out of 10 where 10 is the worst I could have). I ignored it for the most part telling myself that most people get headaches throughout the week. That year, my headaches became more frequent and more intense and I got bronchitis four times.

After college graduation and as my wedding drew closer, I started my first full-time marketing job. I quickly realized that during school I had been better at controlling my body's ups and downs. Now I just had to push through the workday no matter what. Ever since puberty, I had had periodic trouble with insomnia and it seemed to be growing worse as well.

During the fall of that year, I had an intense migraine that caused me to see spots with pain shooting down my neck. My pain stayed at a level of 7 for about a week, compared to the level 2 pain I usually had experienced in college. I went to my general practitioner but he dismissed it as a "pinched nerve" and I laid flat on my back for three days taking muscle relaxants. As the pain subsided, I then got back to my daily routine and took Excedrin on a daily basis to get through the week.

I kept busy the next few months with my new responsibilities of wife and employee, while also helping friends with several weddings and planning various showers on the weekends. My headaches throughout the week were growing in intensity to a level 4 or 5 and I was experiencing a migraine about once a week. In July of the next year at age 23, I had migraines every day leading up to my best friend's wedding and the week after that. The next weekend, while celebrating my husband's birthday, the pain began running down my neck and left arm. This is when it became clear to me that there was a very serious problem and I needed to look into it.

I started out going to a chiropractor, who saw some "minor

problems – nothing serious" in my neck. This caused us to seek a second opinion from an orthopedic surgeon who studied my x-rays and MRI and found a slightly bulging disc. This too did not look like it was affecting the nervous system but he treated it to make sure. After weeks of muscle relaxants (3 times a day), anti–inflammatories, and traction on my neck, I was experiencing no relief. When my doctor suggested we keep up the regimen, I became very emotional and I was filled with resistance. I had been walking around for weeks in a daze and in tremendous pain. Next, he suggested steroid injections in my neck. He did that twice and there was little change in my pain levels. We then went to go see a different chiropractor. He analyzed my x-rays and found that there were, once again some, minor issues but nothing that should be causing me the level of pain I was having. He suggested I look into autoimmune problems.

I then went to a neurologist, who diagnosed me with "pain threshold disorder," which he likened to fibromyalgia or chronic fatigue syndrome. I was thrilled just to have a diagnosis . . . any diagnosis! He then put me on anti-depressants to help with the pain and told me to learn to relax. After a couple months of anti-depressants with little pain relief and serious side-effects that added to my discomfort, he tried an anti-seizure medication. This medication did not decrease my pain but added intense feelings of "pins and needles" and "fire" in my hands and feet. After trying this for three months, the suggested solution was just to combine the two drugs, which I was not willing to do.

I was left scared and getting weaker by the day. My husband and I decided that I should quit my job because of my body's weakened state. At this point, I was spending nights and weekends in bed and using all my energy for work; I wasn't sure how much longer I would even be able to do that. My pain level was staying at about an 8 most of the time. We also discovered throughout this process that I was having high blood pressure and no medication would bring it down. After having many expensive tests run, I was told that everything was "normal" with no explanation concerning my blood pressure. We also noticed that my hair had begun to fall out. I noticed large amounts of my hair in the shower every day.

I had spent a great deal of time in prayer about my condition and one day it occurred to me that my pain intensified during my period week. I began to wonder if there might be a *hormonal* correlation. I had always had cycle problems since I began menstruating at the age of nine. This was also when some insomnia and periodic neck and back pain began. I remembered that a friend of mine had Interstitial Cystitis and found relief through a hormonal treatment with a doctor in Texas. That night at church services, her mom and I found each other wanting to talk about the same thing – Dr. Roby. She gave me directions to his Web site (www.robyinstitute.com) and as soon as my husband and I got home, we looked him up. So many of the people he treated had symptoms that were similar to mine. I called him the next day and he spoke with me at length concerning my symptoms. My symptoms seemed to make sense to him! That day we booked plane tickets to Austin.

When we got to his office, I gave them my extensive health history and they began testing various vials of drops under my tongue. Some vials had no effect, some caused instant pain, and others caused instant ease of the pain and muscle tension. The blood work showed my hormone levels in most cases were actually high, especially my testosterone levels. The high levels of hormones were not a problem but my body had developed allergic reactions to my hormones. I had low cortisol levels, which caused my body to rely on adrenalin. This constant flow of adrenalin was causing my inability to sleep, my hair to fall out, my high blood pressure, and pain with muscle tightness. The low cortisol levels were also decreasing my body's ability to handle stimuli of any kind. I had developed bad environmental allergies, some food allergies, and my hormonal allergies. Dr. Roby put me on a walking regimen to burn off my adrenalin and to allow me to rest as well as giving me some adrenalin drops to help deal with the pain. I place the drops under my tongue and I can feel relief in just a few seconds. He also started me on estrogen blocker drops as well as progesterone blocker drops to desensitize me. Later, we would tweak the strength of the drops to increase the results I was getting along with adding a testosterone blocker vial.

I am 25 years old and it has been six months since I started my treatment. I feel like myself again. My body has been slow to rebalance and I think it will take a couple more months for the problem to be completely corrected. Right now, I am at 90% with periodic headaches that last about 30 minutes and the occasional more severe headache that is about 2 or 3 on the pain scale which are usually remedied when

I take a small dose of pain medication. However, I am still improving and my life has completely turned around. I just started dance lessons for the first time in my life and am able to clean my house again! Before, if I would clean my bathtub or floor, I would be in bed for a couple of days, and my insomnia has improved tremendously. The rest I am now getting has allowed my body to continue to heal. I now physically and emotionally feel up to making plans with my husband, friends, and family and live a normal life.

Don – Arthritis

At 49 years old, I was a healthy, energetic, athletic, and hard working guy and in a flash, my life was dramatically changed. I suffered a stroke that left my entire right side with no feeling whatsoever. Fortunately, after several weeks in a rehab hospital in Charlotte, NC, I was able to learn to walk, to talk, and to take care of myself once again. I knew, however, I would never sing and play my guitar again. I could live with that because I was better off than most of those who I met in rehab. There was one problem, however, that kept lingering. There was a severe pain in my right leg and foot that would not go away no matter what the doctors in rehab had me do. They admitted that this was not typical in a stroke victim and had no recommendation for me that would lower the level of pain I had, let alone get rid of it. The pain I lived with on a day-to-day basis was at a level of 7 to 8 on a scale from 1 to 10.

Regardless of what the doctors at rehab told us, my wife Peggy was determined to find someone to help me. Over the next two years, she took me to a variety of doctors: a chiropractor, who determined my spine was crooked; a physical therapist, who said my muscles were cramping because I was favoring my weaker side; an acupuncturist, who had some pretty weird theories about treatment; a neurosurgeon, who said the two sides of my brain did not connect together anymore; several pain management doctors, who injected my back on every office visit; and various other specialists with one fitting me for a foot and leg brace because he noticed I was walking crooked. By this time, I had back pain that was hitting between a 9 and 10 almost daily. A second neurosurgeon decided I needed a spinal cord stimulator implant (a fancy TENS unit surgically implanted in the spine) which he said could only help the leg but not my foot. Even this would have been great news, but he put it in my back and it didn't help either. I had pretty much resigned myself to a life full of pain and misery, having no hope that the medical field would ever be able to do anything for me. Then a stroke of good fortune happened to us seemingly by accident.

In 1996, Peggy and I were driving through our town and she happened to see a sign saying, "ALLERGY." She suggested that we should stop and maybe at least I could get help with my runny nose, which had been bothering me for some time. Neither of us knew very much about allergies, except that Mountain Cedar fever is pretty bad in Texas and causes a number of people problems during particular seasons. The place we stopped was the Roby Institute and there we met Dr. Russell Roby.

Dr. Roby sat down with us and began explaining to us all about allergies and asking a bunch of questions. Peggy tells the story of our first encounter with Dr. Roby this way: "As Dr. Roby began asking Don about his stroke, he seemed way too interested in his leg and foot pain for an allergy doctor. I was becoming increasingly skeptical, thinking that we had found yet another quack who was going to do something stranger than all the other doctors had tried. I was tempted to just raise my hand, tell him that we are here for his allergies, and tell him to stop talking about Don's stroke. The more we went on, the more I began to get really upset. Then, to top it all off, he pulled out a tray of little vials filled with clear liquids and began to squirt a little of the liquid under Don's tongue. Of course, we had no idea what was in these bottles and found our presence there more and more uncomfortable. After each set of drops, Dr. Roby would ask Don how his leg pain was – 'better, worse, or about the same.' I was just about ready to scream when it happened. On about the fifth vial, Don stood up and walked around. Then, he started dancing around the room. He then broke down and he cried."

Yes, as you might guess, I was extremely emotional. My leg, my foot, and my back were completely free of pain for the first time since the stroke almost 14 years earlier. To me, this was nothing short of a true miracle that I could a) be pain free, b) have it happen so quickly after all the years I had suffered, and c) that none of the other many doctors and specialists I had consulted could do anything for me. I remember, interestingly, that Dr. Roby just kept taking notes as if this is what he had fully expected to happen.

Since that day, I have told this story to other doctors. They smile and say, "I am happy for you." I know they don't believe me, because they never even ask questions. But this event in my life is such a miracle that I want everybody to know. In all these years, the pain in my leg and foot has never returned. Occasionally, the pain in my back returns, but after being tested in Dr. Roby's office, I have discovered that I am extremely allergic to almost everything out-of-doors. When the different allergens come my way and the symptoms return, I head to the Roby Institute. Each time I go and come out feeling whole again, I cannot help but remember that very first day we walked into his office for allergies and received relief for pains that had been plaguing me for 14 years. I think about what my life would be like today if we had not stopped. Thank heaven we did.

GlaDíenne – Fibromyalgia, Panic Disorder, Asthma

My journey to Dr. Roby and the Roby Institute was a long, extremely painful and often humiliating one. I will soon be 64 years old, I have four children and 14 grandchildren, and my story shows that it is never too late to get help. By the time I found my way to Dr. Roby, my body was like a train wreck.

When I was 21, I was diagnosed with hypothyroidism and my thyroid gland had practically ceased to function. The doctor put me on Armour Thyroid, a natural thyroid, but at some point in the process, another doctor put me on a synthetic thyroid, keeping me at the low end of "normal." Through the years, they never checked my free T3 to determine whether my thyroid was functioning properly, so I was just limping along with a very low thyroid level. I also had weight problems as well as all the other problems that come with low thyroid. By the time I was 25, I had four children I was left to raise alone. I call these years of my life the "Dark Years of Medicine." The medical doctors were awful; no dignity or respect for women. I was put on all kinds of medications, including antidepressants. The doctor said "Well, you're divorced with four children; if you're not depressed, you should be." I told him I was sick and tired of being tired and sick. My life was a total mess and as if that was not enough, the surgeries started (appendix, gall bladder, uterus, and ovaries).

I had terrible migraine headaches that would put me down for an entire day at a time. I developed Irritable Bowel Syndrome (IBS), asthma, and other allergies. I was allergic to all pain medications, so I could only take aspirin or Ibuprofen. I do have a high pain tolerance (thank God for that) but the over-the-counter pain medications didn't really help that much. Consequently, I just had to suffer. By the time I was 40 years old, I had cancer of the vaginal wall. At age 41, I had developed a mass on my left ovary and at 43, they removed my right ovary as well. I was put on hormone replacement until the age of 58 when they took me off the hormones. That is when I really took a nosedive.

I apparently have had fibromyalgia since my 20's and this was before anyone even knew what to call it. Rather than to continue to suffer the humiliation of doctors telling me it "is all in your head" (like I was crazy), I learned to suffer in silence. In self-defense, in my early 40's I learned to read and study about alternative methods of treating my various problems, including taking many vitamins and supplements. I had my own Physician's Desk Reference (PDR) so I could read up on side effects of and interactions between the various medications that had been prescribed for me. I also learned to say "No!" to any new medications, because I was already taking so many. I lived all over the country, always trying to find a new doctor that could help me.

Although I had been verbally, physically, and mentally abused by so many of my medical doctors, it was still necessary for me to go at least once per year to have blood work done because of my hypothyroidism. Just the anxiety of what the next one would do to me would put me into posttraumatic stress syndrome. However, I remarried when I was 42 to John, a truly wonderful man, who would always go with me to at least make sure they were not ugly to me. For the last four years (since age 60), I have been bedridden for three to four months at a time because of the severe pain from the fibromyalgia and also a degenerative disc problem. Because of the fibromyalgia, my balance was affected and I often fall, one time in the bathtub breaking the ribs on my left side to add to my pain and suffering.

In 2007, we moved back to Austin, Texas because I had been

unable to find a doctor who could help me; I simply did not know where to turn and no answers were appearing on the horizon. Then, during a period when I had been in bed for five months, a friend called from another city and told me what she had learned about Dr. Roby. I called to make the appointment and provided a little of my history over the phone. The woman on the other end of the line said my circumstances sounded like hers before she found Dr. Roby. Cautiously, I began to feel some sense of hope.

In order for Dr. Roby's office to get a true reading on me, I had to go off any medication I was taking for pain; this included antihistamines for allergies and panic disorder medication. I was in so much pain I could hardly walk; everything hurt except my eyelids and I cried all the way through my first two appointments. Dr. Roby ultimately told me that I probably had been born with a hormone imbalance . . . and he assured me I would get well. They performed additional allergy testing, finding I now was allergic to sugar, tomatoes, oranges, and chocolate, besides the other allergies of which I was already aware. They ordered blood work for my free T3 and all hormones.

The results were astounding! My levels were comparable to a woman between 80 and 100 years old. You will never know how wonderful it was to know finally that I wasn't crazy. I knew down deep I wasn't, but when you have all these doctors telling you that there is really nothing wrong with you, it causes you to wonder. I was indeed sick and there was real reason for all the pain and suffering that I had been enduring for years. No wonder I was a physical and emotional mess!

They started me on Armour Thyroid, compounded estrogen, and testosterone, along with progesterone and thyroid drops to spray under my tongue. I had to take extra Vitamin C, B-Complex, and a supplement to help heal my adrenal glands that were basically shot. I was told not to watch exciting TV programs or anything that would produce stress or anxiety. I was to do slow rhythmic movements for exercise. And for my diet, I was put on a combination of "Sugar Busters" and "Dr. Atkins." Additionally, Dr. Roby told me to make a journal, writing down each day all my medications and supplements. I also checked and recorded my blood pressure in the morning and evening. After six weeks, they took another blood panel and my body was not accepting the thyroid and estrogen as it should. They needed to separate the progesterone, estrogen, and thyroid drops to spray under my tongue to get my 64-year-old body to recognize the thyroid and estrogen and start using it.

I noticed improvement almost immediately and my friends noticed how strong my voice was on the phone. Prior to my trip to Dr. Roby, I had not been able to reach my right arm around to hook my bra for about a year, but within six weeks, I could hook my own bra. Within three months, I had lost 28 pounds. At Christmas, I went to a party and was up dancing with a 19-year-old young man and keeping up with him. Three months before, I had been in a wheel chair on a trip to Florida because I couldn't walk in the airport. I feel like I am a walking miracle.

What Dr. Roby does is so cutting edge that I am confident that no other doctor would have known what to do when my body wasn't recognizing the thyroid, estrogen, and the need to separate the progesterone and estrogen drops so there would be no side effects. For the first time ever, I can touch my legs without deep agonizing pain. Without Dr. Roby and his wonderful staff at the Roby Institute, I would still be an invalid. I have always looked much younger than I really was and now, thanks to Dr. Roby and his incredible work, my 64-year-old insides are matching up to my younger outsides. I have been given the gift of life without pain. Thanks to Dr. Roby, I am literally coming back from the dead, and if someone like I can do this, you who are reading this book can do it, too.

Julie – Arthritis, Allergies, Asthma, Migraine Headaches, and PMS

I'm going to try to describe my life history of being incarnated in a body that just seems to want to be chronically sick. Having a high value for health (being a Pilates instructor), I am very sad to say that I have not had many days in my life where I have felt well.

Let me start by saying that when I was a child, I was sick virtually all of the time. By the time I was three months old, I was given my first antibiotics and from that time forward up until about the time I was 17, I have been continually on antibiotics. I grew up on the Oregon coast, a pretty cold and moldy place, so it seemed like I constantly had some sort of infection. These were usually ear, nose, and throat infections and I later came to realize that I pretty much had chronic Candida. Multiple yeast infections made me feel ill or kind of like I was getting the flu all of the time. I was out of school more than I was in school and was frequently visiting doctors. This was extremely distressing to my mother and me because as a child it was difficult for me to describe how I felt. When I was about seven years old, I told the doctor that I felt like a rotten tomato. He thought that was very funny, but coming from a farming background, that was the only thing that came to me – I just felt ill practically all the time.

Also, as a child I had chronic aching from head to toe, like a mild fever. I remember at night feeling very cold with every joint in my body aching; the doctors used to say that was the flu. I can't imagine that you could have the flu that much, but that is what they said. So it was antibiotics on top of antibiotics until around nine years old, I was diagnosed with asthma. They didn't have a lot of things to treat asthma back then, but from that time forward I've been on various inhalers and nasal sprays and of course prednisone a couple times a year when it would get really bad. The cycle used to start with sinus infections or ear infections, go into chest distress and asthma, and then cycle back around to ear, nose, and throat infections. Then I would cycle down into bronchitis where I'm coughing my lungs out sometimes for months at a time. Doctors thought I was crazy, making it up, or just lying to get out of school or work, when actually I was just very, very ill. Nobody knew what to do. I think the doctors just couldn't buck up and face the fact that they just didn't have an answer.

I guess I could have lived with that story if it had ended there, but another thing that went along with this was some sort of chronic indigestion. I pretty much have lived on Alka-Seltzer twice a day for maybe 20 years to try to settle down my stomach. Because of the chronic aching, I would use a whole store full of Tylenol and Ibuprofen and over the counter things to try to stomp down the aching in my joints. At different stages of my life, I had three different doctors say that they believed my symptoms pointed to lupus, which was a very scary thing to hear. They would do the test and I didn't have lupus. The other thing they kept telling me is I must have chronic fatigue syndrome. Those symptoms, as well as the lupus symptoms, seemed to match what I was experiencing.

Ultimately, I was looking for somebody I thought might know

something in alternative medicine and give me an accurate diagnosis. I found a Chinese doctor, a woman in California (who turned out to be a regular M.D.), and she told me I had rheumatoid arthritis. She started treating me for that with a bunch of drugs that didn't help and even made me worse. All the while, I am trying to keep my chin up and not let people know I'm ill. It takes a lot of energy to put a smile on your face and act well when inside you're, you know, you're just sick. It is a pretty miserable existence.

Another problem at the top of my list is allergies. I've moved a good bit and each time I move, I get hit with a whole bunch of new strains of something. I'm used to mold coming from Oregon, but now that I was in Austin, I had this big problem with Mountain Cedar. Other things were starting to pop up, and an allergist I had gone to gave me the same old antibiotics and an inhaler. Typically, I will get a little small infection or I'll be coughing or my body will start aching, and I just have that feeling that I'm about to get the flu or something; but I know something is wrong. In the past when that happens, within 24 hours I'm so sick that I just expect that I'm going to be sick for three months. I did try some other kind of things that bordered on voodoo or hocus-pocus sort of things, none of which helped me. I was still sick and at a loss for anything that would give me any relief until just a few months ago when I decided to go to the Roby Institute. I took this step to go to Dr. Roby because my husband had had some success with his allergies there. I took notice that he was getting a little better, and a little better, and I finally decided to follow suit. I had tried everything else possible, so I figured why not.

I went in and it was very strange. I sat down and talked to someone and she squirted something under my tongue, which was like salt water. Believe it or not, within a few seconds, I felt better. I thought, "This is weird; I'm just making this up. This can't be true." With my history with doctors, I was the consummate skeptic; but after having had so many things fail, I just decided to wait and see and give them a chance. I got started on this program, and I have to say that even though I don't understand what is happening, I can say that it is truly working. I don't know why it's working and sometimes I still have to stop and ask myself if I'm making this up or if this is some placebo.

The worst situation for me is when my symptoms cycle into a migraine headache. For me I don't think there is anything worse than having a migraine. The second I start getting that little halo feeling, I start getting distressed; I start seeing spots, things get a little blurry, and I know exactly what is going to happen. My body starts to overheat, I start to panic, and in the past, I would have to tell you, that the next three days of my life are just the most insanely horrible thing to go through. For someone who has never had a migraine I won't even bother trying to explain it, but it is not a normal headache. A normal headache, I can buck up and live with, but this is like I would rather just end my life.

Four days ago, I started to have that little halo and seeing spots. The first thing I did was call on my cell phone to tell Dr. Roby that I was starting to have some symptoms. He worked with me on the phone as we went through using things he had given me in these vials. My headache gradually went from a 9 (on a scale of 1–10) to a 7 to a 5 to a 3 or 4, and finally to about a 2. I felt still a little queasy so I went to bed and took a nap. I did call in and cancel my clients the next day. That is also a new trick I am learning from Dr. Roby; take a little time off and it pretty much saves your life. So I did that; I canceled my morning clients, I went to bed, and relaxed. I went into work about noon the next day and my headache was virtually gone. And now, it is four days later and I have to say that I feel perfectly fine. I have been practicing this protocol that I learned from Dr. Roby enough so that I can write it down and sort of get myself through. If I forget what to do, I can call either him or one of his assistants and they are extremely helpful to try to work through which vials I'm going to use to try to treat my symptoms by myself. It can be a little confusing, but it is nice to have somebody there to help you when in fact your brain is slowing down and you can't think very straight.

Lastly, I will mention my biggest challenge and my big life-wrecker: PMS. At the time of this writing, I am now exploring the probability that my progesterone allergy triggers the severe emotional roller coaster that has sent me into a predictable psychotic fit of hysteria (since about the age of 13) every 20 days or so. My symptoms seem to be subsiding a little more each month, and I am finding that I am less and less threatened by my own menstrual cycle.

All of this is astonishing to me based on looking backwards in my life and pretty much having my whole identity wrapped up in being a closet sick person. I have felt defective or actually embarrassed about being sick all the time. What I heard through my whole childhood was that I was making this up. I just know that what Dr. Roby does works. I don't have lupus; I don't have chronic fatigue syndrome; and I don't have rheumatoid arthritis. I used to have five, six, seven infections a year with a bottle of antibiotics attached to each one of those as I cycled through. No more. I haven't had even one this year. I have more hope than I think I've ever had a day in my life. I'm very excited. I am clueless; it is not as if I really understand what I'm doing, but given my history, I am the first in line to let people coach me so I can learn how to live a better life and feel great doing it.

Lori – Allergy and Hormone Imbalance

My journey to Dr. Roby was a long, agonizing one and I suffered in pain for almost two years before I found him. It began in January 2006 when I went to my primary doctor for a routine checkup and to have my anxiety medications refilled. I suffered from anxiety for many years and was treated with an anti-anxiety drug to help with sleep and the shaking of my hands. While I was there, he decided it was time for me to receive an updated tetanus shot since I hadn't had one since I was a child, and since I was 34, he thought I should have it updated. After receiving the shot, my life as I knew it went down in flames.

Within two months, my aches and pains began. They started in my shoulder and I was referred to an orthopedic surgeon for examination. He concluded that it may be a rotator cuff problem and proceeded to give me a cortisone shot. The shot did help with my shoulder but then the unrelenting pain spread all over my entire body. By April 2006, I was diagnosed with fibromyalgia by my primary doctor. He sent me to a rheumatologist for confirmation of the diagnosis. They were in agreement and I was told that my primary doctor would be able to control my pain with medications. He prescribed several different anti-depressants, which my body was unable to tolerate, and suggested that I see his in-house counselor. After several visits to his counselor, she concluded that I was "not crazy," I was just in pain and needed to be given something for it.

My primary doctor then prescribed narcotics and muscle relaxers to try and help control the all-over body pain that I was having. The treatment received was not helping my pain. It got to the point where I was unable to go into work and was only able to work from home. Then, the search began to find someone to relieve my pain and help me return to my normal life. All in all, I saw 27 doctors: rheumatologists, neurologists, doctors at pain management clinics, podiatrists, chiropractors, gynecologists, homeopathic doctors, and yes, even an Amish doctor. Almost all of them had a remedy they had chosen, but none of them were able to alleviate my pain. I had blood test after blood test; I had MRIs, x-rays, EMGs, heavy metal testing, and nerve conduction studies done sometimes more than once. All the tests that I had came back absolutely normal!! This left me to believe that I was crazy and that there was no hope for me ever feeling like myself again. Some recommended massage therapy, which helped for about 24 hours; some suggested vitamin supplements; and one even had me try intravenous chelation therapy to rid my body of heavy metals. Many suggested that the pain was all in my head, so to test that theory, I went to two hypnotherapists both of which were unable to convince my head that I was not in pain.

During all of this, I continued to seek treatment from my primary doctor who had continued to prescribe the narcotics, muscle relaxers, and sleep aids that helped some but did not take my pain away; it only decreased the intensity of it. My husband and I decided to take a trip to Florida, and to our surprise, my pain went away within just a few days of being there. We were unable to find the reason for it but decided that maybe we should get a place there on the beach so that I would be able to go there and recover from time to time. This plan worked pain-wise, but it took me away from my family including my husband who had to stay in Ohio to run our two automobile dealerships. I spent a lot of time there isolated and away from my family so I could keep my pain at bay.

In July of 2007, they came out with a new drug that was to treat fibromyalgia patients called Lyrica. This excited me and I made a trip back to Ohio to see my primary doctor and request that I get this new drug. He went ahead and prescribed it, but it too failed to relieve my pain. In disappointment, I went back to Florida to get some relief from the pain. At that point, I decided that the only way that I was going to have any relief from the pain was to stay there, alone. My husband was able to visit when he could get away, but being away from him was agonizing. He also didn't want me to return to Ohio and live in the pain that I had to endure while there. So I stayed that year, even through the holidays, and I was unable to go home and be with my family. Being away from my family for the holidays was another turning point for me, so I began a search for someone once again to help me.

That is when I ran across Dr. Roby's Web site. His Web site was so informative that I had to call and get an appointment to see him. His approach was like no other that I had ever run across. The allergy and hormone route is the one that I had never taken. None of my 27 doctors had ever recommended that this testing be done. My appointment was for the first week of February 2008. While making the long drive to Austin, my pain seemed to increase by the mile and by the time I arrived in Austin, I was a total mess, pain head to toe. Thoughts ran through my mind that night that this has got to be the dumbest thing I have ever done. I wasn't even sure how I was going to drive back to Florida if his approach didn't work.

What I'm trying to say is that I was the biggest skeptic in the world when it came to doctors at this point. I woke up the morning of my appointment in such pain that I could hardly drive to Dr. Roby's office. When I arrived, my pain level in most areas of my body was at a 7 or more. They began testing with the drops and my pain began to go down after only a few of the various drops were given to me. Within the few hours that I was in his office, my pain was gone. All of it!! Dr. Roby found out that the labs that I had done prior to going to Austin showed that many of my hormones were low. He also found out through allergy testing that I had allergies that I never even knew I had, which explained why I felt better in Florida. The clean ocean air was alleviating my symptoms since there were no allergens to fight. With the drops he was able to not only relieve the pain that I had but he was also able to relieve the constant shake that I had experienced in my hands for so many years. They prepared the drops that I would need overnight; I picked them up the next day and was able to return to Ohio. Still being the skeptic, I wanted to see if the drops would work where I was unable to be pain free before, in Ohio.

Well, it's been about 90 days now as I write this, and I'm still pain free. I don't take any of the pain meds anymore, nor the Lyrica, nor the muscle relaxers . . . nothing, except the drops and creams that Dr. Roby told me to take. Guess it wasn't what the doctors had diagnosed me with so many times. I didn't have fibromyalgia; I simply had allergies and hormone imbalances. I'm so thankful that I found Dr. Roby and thankful that because of his approach, I will get my life back. It will still take some time for my body to recover from the damage it incurred with lack of movement during my times of pain, but it will repair itself with the things that I learned from Dr. Roby. With the drops, exercise, and proper diet, I have faith that I will get my life back!

Dorothy – Migraines and Behcet's Disease

In 1989, I was diagnosed with vulvar cancer. This was rubber stamped by another gynecologist and subsequently, a GYN oncologist. It was decided that I would try chemotherapy, before resorting to surgery. Unfortunately, the chemo did nothing but make me sicker and even caused liver enzyme problems. Between 1989 and 1991, there were more surgeries, including two to correct the botches of the others. I developed apthous ulcers, vaginal ulcers, and an ulcerative colon. Although the surgeons told me that the only remedy was surgery, I said "no." I was reluctant to take the drugs that they prescribed (Plaquenil, methotrexate, thalidomide, and prednisone) because the side effects were even worse than the supposed disease state.

I was tested for every disease that any infectious disease specialist could think of and my condition continued to worsen. Now, there were other symptoms . . . I was grossly swollen; I had red, throbbing joints and unexplainable rashes; I experienced three- and four-day debilitating migraines; I was extremely depressed . . . the list went on and on. In 1991, they decided that I had lupus; when I pointed out that the symptoms were inconsistent with lupus, it was quickly changed to Sjogren's Syndrome, and when I didn't like that one either, to Behcet's Disease/Syndrome. They carefully explained that it was a particularly nasty little disease that no one really knew anything about, except that it would be fatal, it would be increasingly painful, there was no known cause and no known cure, that I had maybe three more years of life, and that in the annals of medicine, there are no records of a Behcet's patient reaching or surpassing, his/her 60th birthday.

Even though I didn't believe the prognosis, my health continued to go downhill. Everything increased in intensity and I was rarely able to leave my home. I was always exhausted, couldn't eat, didn't sleep, and had almost constant migraines. I decided that I hated all of the doctors on my case, and that I would just give up and die in peace. Since I had no life and no hope of getting better, there wasn't much point of being in the world of hurt.

In 1994, one of my friends was a nurse in Dr. Roby's office. She pushed me to see him because, as she said, "I've seen how Dr. Roby has helped so many other desperate people to get well when no other doctor had been able to." I refused to go. I hated all doctors by then and was not going to see another. A few days later, my friend called at a time when I was so sick with a migraine that I couldn't get out of bed. She told me that Dr. Roby was sending her to pick me up to take me to his office, and she would see me in 10 minutes. She threatened to call the suicide squad if I didn't answer the door. I agreed to see him just to stop her harassment.

When Dr. Roby entered the exam room where I had been placed, we actually just chatted for quite a while. He explained his protocol, told me why he thought in that way, talked about his years of research and the results he had experienced. I am the ultimate cynic, but I was in such pain that he could have offered to chop me into little pieces, and I would have agreed to try it if it would stop the pain. He explained that he wanted to put a couple of substances under my skin to see if he could see what I was reacting to. I have always been allergic and was comfortable with the process. I did, however, make him aware that I was reacting to everything, and everything made me get worse. He asked me to quantify my headache on a scale of 0, meaning no pain, to 10, meaning the worst possible pain. My only choices were worse, better, or the same. I thought that my pain was about 85, but had to settle for a 10.

The first one that he used did not make me worse or better, which was a bit of a surprise. When he injected the second substance, it was an even bigger surprise. Within less than 10 seconds, I could feel things moving around inside my skull, and I could feel the headache sort of gently going away. I just couldn't believe that it was happening. In less than half a minute, my three- or four-day headache was gone . . . completely. I was so stunned that I didn't realize that the ulcers in my mouth were gone also; the pains in my joints were gone; all of the swelling in my body was gone. I just couldn't believe it! When he offered to reverse the "cure" and bring it back, I agreed to that, as well. He brought it back and then made it go away, again. I was convinced!

I have been his patient since then, and I credit his care with keeping me alive. I have never had another migraine. Even though I sometimes still have allergy headaches, or tension headaches, or even dehydration headaches, I do not have the unremitting agony of migraines. I am now 70 years old and without any of the symptoms that were causing my long, slow, and painful "death in three years" promised by conventional medicine.

Beth – Tachycardia

Dr. Russell Roby has been my allergy doctor since 1994. I have many airborne allergies and have had severe reactions to prescription medications. About 10 years ago, my family doctor discovered I had high blood pressure. He tried six different types of medications before finding one I could tolerate without reactions and that would work to lower my blood pressure. I have been on Atenolol to keep this under control ever since.

About 2001, I began having problems with tachycardia. If I was really upset, it was guaranteed my heart would race. The puzzle was that I often woke from a sound sleep with my heart pounding. I felt like I had run for miles. I could be sitting in the movies perfectly calm and my heart would take off. Feeling your heart race at 140-150 beats a minute is very frightening. Over the next three years, I went to six different cardiologists. I had thousands of dollars in testing done: EKGs, echocardiography, treadmill tests, tilt table tests, and many others were done as well. The doctors could not find what was wrong. I went to a doctor in San Antonio for a different treadmill test and tried to wear a Holter monitor. I was allergic to the tape they used and had to give that up after 48 hours. At one point, my heart was racing so fast and blood pressure went so high, I was told by my cardiologist to go to Austin Heart Hospital. They had me chew aspirin and gave me an IV of something until things were under control. I was then sent home still with no answers!

The last cardiologist I saw in Austin wanted to do a stress test with dye and I scheduled the appointment for the test. Because I have had such severe allergic reactions, I was very nervous about a reaction to this dye! I found out about Dr. Roby, called him, and he told me he knew what was wrong with me . . . and not to have this test. He told me to come to his office and let him try drops under my tongue. Dr. Roby sent me home with a vial of epinephrine after determining the right strength. He told me to take these drops under my tongue each day and call him to let him know if I had any more problems. He also said to walk 20 minutes daily. Let's see . . . have surgery, or try drops under my tongue . . . let me think!

It has been four years since I started taking epinephrine daily and have returned to a normal life. No more racing heart! My cardiologist said this would not work and I said it is working!! I cancelled my treadmill stress test with him and was told I was risking a heart attack! They said giving adrenalin to someone for a racing heart was absolutely CRAZY! I was told Dr. Roby was crazy! Oh, and did they know his name? My family physician was horrified as well. He told me I was risking my life and that epinephrine would absolutely not work. Also, he said that Atenolol and epinephrine would counteract each other and I would have high blood pressure problems again (I don't!).

Again, it is working; I have no more tachycardia and my blood pressure is under control! How can anyone argue with that? Who would think to go to their allergy doctor for heart problems? Perhaps more people should!

Gerry – Idiopathic Pulmonary Fibrosis (IPF)

I was diagnosed in 2003 with a heart condition. I was going into atrial fibrillation about every two or three days. The doctors at the heart hospital in Austin tried several drugs and electro cardioversions to bring me into a normal rhythm. After nine such attempts, I was placed on amiodarone for several months. It is not recommended by the FDA for atrial fibrillation, but I was placed on it anyway. I was also taking Coumadin and going in frequently for blood work to make sure that the dosage was correct. After a month or so on amiodarone, I started telling the nurse that I was having trouble breathing. Finally, one day I reported to her that I had no energy and could hardly catch my breath and I began to cry. She made an appointment with my cardiologist at that time.

I was eventually scheduled for a procedure called ablation where they cauterize in the area of the extra impulses in my heart to try to correct the extreme arrhythmia. It was unsuccessful. Then I had an arteriogram and they discovered that I had an insufficient mitral valve that was not closing. This resulted in an enlarged heart.

I was advised that a different surgeon would do the valve repair and he also performed the maze technique (I think that is another type of ablation). After being in ICU for a few days, they put me into a regular room. My heart was stopping, so next thing I knew, I was on the table again for a pacemaker.

Although my heart seemed to be working better, my breathing was not. The surgeon put me on prednisone and I experienced every known side effect for that medicine. Finally, he sent me to a pulmonologist and let him wean me from the prednisone. My first visit was in December of 2004 and after reviewing my records, he immediately diagnosed idiopathic pulmonary fibrosis (IPF).

I had never heard of such a disease and when I asked for the prognosis, he said "You have about five years to live." Needless to say, my heart was broken. He also advised me to get my house in order, so I went home, cried a lot for a year or so, worked on my will, and informed my friends and family. In March of 2005, I had the IPF diagnosis confirmed by an open lung biopsy. Following this, I was informed that my prognosis was changed to "You may live two years." I was devastated as was my husband of 47 years, my two daughters, and my six grandchildren, not to mention all my friends and the rest of my family. I went to Tulane to try to get into an experimental program. I was not acceptable because of the rapid decline in my condition and my age. I was 65 years old at the time. I was able to get the drug they were testing at a monthly cost of over $5000. However, there is now a class action suit against the drug manufacturer since the medicine had no benefits and they had falsified claims. By December 2007, I realized I had outlived the doctors' expectations. However, my breathing was getting worse all the time. I had gone from 2 liters per minute (lpm) of oxygen to 8+ and I had been on oxygen for three years, 24/7.

One day my husband, a doctor in Austin, came home and told me he had made an appointment with a Dr. Roby. I asked why. He said,

"What have you got to lose? Nothing." So I reluctantly went to see this new physician. I had no hope of him being able to do anything. Surely, if there was any way to make my life better, someone would have tried to help me, right? Dr. Roby had me walk down the hallway with his nurse by my side and without my oxygen. When I walked into his office, my saturation was 78%. I sat down and he had his nurse spritz something under my tongue and with my oxygen off, my saturation went up to 92%. I could see it with my own eyes. My husband was amazed.

Dr. Roby proceeded to try different meds under my tongue, and he also tested me for allergies. Guess what. I am allergic to cedar, mesquite, cow hair, and dust (to name a few). I live on a ranch outside of town and the place is covered with all of those trees, cows, and dust.

I am now living. I have hope for the future. I take my medicines daily and am now breathing without the aid of an oxygen concentrator most of the time. At night, I am sleeping with 2 lpm. This is truly unbelievable! My husband admitted to me that, before we went to see Dr. Roby, he truly had felt I would not survive the summer, since I was declining so rapidly.

Dr. Roby also checked my hormone levels. I am 68 and have such low levels for some hormones that this probably contributed to the heart problems, since I had nothing to balance the stress and adrenalin surges. I am now replacing estrogen, testosterone, and DHEA and taking daily sublingual doses for my allergies. I tried a treadmill last week and was able to walk for 15 minutes at a slow speed, but I can build myself up by concentrating on a healthy life style of good food and exercise and putting my body in balance with hormone replacements.

I am so excited! I feel like I have been given a miracle! Dr. Roby's knowledge and abilities have given me a new lease on life. I can never thank him enough for the care, time, and expertise he has given me. It is truly a miracle!

Chapter 4

Complementary and Alternative Medicine

Frequently, patients will ask me if I would be willing to share this information with their doctors and I tell them that we have shared this with their doctors . . . or doctors like them. This information is offered with complete instructions; all you have to do is read it and do it. It is available; we are not selling it, we are giving it away. I have presented this information several times at medical meetings including the American College of Allergy, Asthma and Immunology (Anaheim, CA., 2005) and two annual meetings of the Pan American Allergy Society (San Antonio, TX., 2004 and Dallas, TX., 2005). I continue to try to share what I am doing with any doctor who expresses an interest or will call me. Doctors are not pleased with this information when my patients try to explain it to them. I tell them their doctors do not care. Not only do they not care, they will try to make you look stupid. Shortly after this book is published, I will have presented this material at a major conference on Complementary and Alternative Medicine. They expect to have 400 or 500 doctors who are interested in Alternative Medicine and I am going to present this very material. Maybe that will do some good, but one must realize that *these* doctors are interested in Alternative Medicine; the vast majority of doctors are not. And you cannot blame them . . . their traditional methods work very well for many of their patients.

I became interested in Complementary and Alternative Medicine when I got so sick as an intern and my doctor tried to convince me I was "fine." He clearly suggested I had a psychiatric disorder . . . it was "all in my head." When I cleared up all my symptoms with diet and exercise, I began to see allergy as a cause of many symptoms. Consequently, I switched out of cardiovascular surgery and started studying adult allergy, run by internal medicine doctors. Unfortunately, they take exactly the same point of view that my doctor did. They do not *believe* in the existence of food allergy. And we are talking about rigidly held *beliefs,* like dictators not *believing* in democracy. That seemed like an incredible proposition to me; how could you not believe in food allergy? Who does not know somebody that reacts when they eat a food?

➢ DOCTORS WHO "BELIEVE"

Nevertheless, I saw that they were not going to have any part of food allergy. The training system for allergists was just an extension of medical school, except we now have more diseases and more drugs, but the same old "connect the dots" approach. But still, no consideration to what might be actually *causing* the problem. From my point of view, I had rapidly come to the conclusion that the cause of my problem was some type of a reaction to food and lack of physical motion. I figured that maybe the pediatricians would know something about this; they deal with babies and surely some of them must have milk allergy. So, I looked at pediatric allergy. I discovered that they, too, do not believe in food allergy. They did not want to hear anything about the fact that children might be intolerant to milk, which seemed to me the most obvious of observations: baby drinks milk, baby throws up. Milk allergy? Oh, no. Pyloric stenosis . . . call the surgeons.

There was only one avenue left: otolaryngology allergy, made up of ear, nose, and throat (ENT) surgeons. Within that group, there was a subset called Rinkel Allergists. Rinkel Allergy began at the University of Michigan in 1939 by Dr. Hansel and Dr. Rinkel, two ENT professors who believed in food allergy. In fact, they developed an entire section of that medical program that dealt exclusively with food allergy and there was a cadre of ENT allergists around the country who followed that line of thinking. I went to the Rinkel training session at a conference known as Pan American Allergy Society. At that meeting, I saw many demonstrations where patients were given *antigens* (substances that produce an allergic response) under their skin and their symptoms were reversed in just a matter of seconds. Regardless of whether the antigen might be food or airborne types, there was an *immediate* relief of symptoms when they injected these antigens under the skin. Needless to say, I was very impressed, because one of the doctors who was demonstrating this showed us that he could make the patient's discomfort come or go seconds apart in sequence simply by adjusting the strength of the antigen that he put under their skin. I found that immensely impressive *and* they believed in food allergy. As a result, I studied that method of treatment, went to their course for a week, and became a member of The Pan American Allergy Society (Dallas, TX., 1974).

I only completed one year of medical training after medical school, because I could not find any area of specialization that I thought would further what I wanted to do. I wanted to explore cases like mine where there seems to be nothing wrong with the patients and yet they experience severe symptoms. I wanted to specialize in illnesses with no proven cause and no known treatment. From that day to this, I have been content to deal with patients who are not sick. *I do not deal with sick patients; medical doctors do that.* However, if patients are told by their doctor that there is nothing wrong with them, then I am perfectly happy to talk with them about how we might explore what might be causing their symptoms and how we can correct that. So, for the last 30 years, I have dealt with what I call "mysterious illnesses." The cornerstone of this is what we already know from their doctors' studies and examination: there is *nothing wrong* with these patients. My patients are sick to death of being told by their doctor that there isn't anything wrong. It would be more acceptable if the doctor admitted he couldn't find anything wrong; but no, he will insist there isn't anything wrong. They are apparently rejecting the patient's description of the terrible symptoms and spend a lot of time trying to convince the patient that there is *nothing* going on, when the patient knows perfectly well there is. These are the patients who come to me and in whom I specialize. You can imagine what happens if I make all their symptoms go away . . . immediately. First surprise, then ANGER.

➢ REVERSING THE PATTERN

The purpose of this book is to try to introduce this information to more and more people a) because it is so simple and b) so that more people can get rid of their symptoms before they ever see a doctor.

For the past many years, the Roby Institute has been a last resort, after patients have explored every other avenue of treatment. My patients frequently come in with six medical specialists in their relatively recent background. There are almost always a gastroenterologist, a rheumatologist, a dermatologist, a neurologist, an OB/GYN, an ENT, a psychiatrist . . . and after everybody has examined the patients, they come to me. After not one of these specialists can find anything wrong, then finally, the patients, through some relative or friend that hears about me or some of the public material that I publish on the Internet or on television, find their way to my door. They come and try what we do and find that the solution is available within moments of the time they come in the office: from neutralization of symptoms to balancing their hormones and/or just the general lifestyle changes we encourage. This book is designed to help people understand that most of these things could be done at home, on their own, before they ever go to a doctor.

I believe half of the patients in any doctor's office might be relieved of most of their symptoms by placing a few drops of progesterone under their tongues. If the drops block your pain or shortness of breath, why would you see the doctor? If we can clear up shortness of breath that lasted seven years, if we can make that go from a level of 10 to a level of 0 in five minutes, if we can show patients how to do this on their own . . . then why would they go to the doctor? If you get rid of your shortness of breath and we show you ways to keep it from coming back, if you get rid of your pain, if you get rid of your itch, if you get rid of whatever is ailing you, then why would you go to the doctor? The purpose of this book and pretty much all that we do is to show patients how they can *avoid* the medical system entirely. If not avoid it, then certainly reverse the pattern that usually occurs where we are the last resort. Come to us first; if we cannot help you (and you will know immediately if it works or not), then you truly are sick and need to see a traditional doctor of some sort. We will happily send you on your way and make recommendations for the types of doctors you should consider. Doctors are terrific at detecting and treating diseases they know. But, they can't help you at all if you don't have one of those diseases they studied.

Exactly what is Complementary and Alternative Medicine (CAM)? A quick visit to the National Institute of Health (NIH) Web site on these practices (http://nccam.nih.gov/health/whatiscam/) will provide you with more than enough detailed information. In short, CAM involves approaches to health care that are outside the realm of conventional medicine. Most medical doctors shun CAM until they find they have no answers to a particular patient's problems. Some use these methods in concert with their traditional medicine practices, and some doctors practice CAM exclusively. As practiced in the United States, CAM is a fairly new concept; actually, it has been around for a long time in the form of chiropractors, naturopaths, homeopaths, and acupuncturists, but it is becoming more and more popular because more and more people have become disenchanted with traditional medicine. A primary difference that some will note between the two (traditional medicine and CAM) is that the former is replete with scientific studies while the latter has fewer of these to back up and confirm what they do.

➢ TREAT THE *CAUSES*, NOT THE SYMPTOMS

Traditional medicine is currently using some powerful chemicals (drugs); most of them are not good for you. They are using some serious antitoxins (poisons) to deal with patients' symptoms. They are not literally trying to poison you, but are relying only on what they know for treatment of your symptoms. Medicine has reached the point where it knows more and more about less and less and it has become *symptom oriented*. If you go to a doctor with a headache, he is going to give you a headache pill. He is not going to sit down and explore your lifestyle to figure out the cause of your headaches. If you come in with fibromyalgia pain, he is going to give you a pain pill or a tranquilizer or both. If you continue to complain, he will prescribe an antidepressant. If you *still* complain, he will double the dose or add a second one. I stated earlier he is not going to sit down and try to figure out the *cause* of the pain. We have the best-trained physicians on earth at detecting and treating diseases; but the conditions we are talking about in this book are not diseases; they are syndromes. They are descriptions of a constellation of symptoms and the more symptoms that are involved, the more the doctor is inclined to feel that the patient is a nut.

As it happens, true medical disease is a pretty narrow

phenomenon. If you have read Shannon Brownlee's book, Overtreated: Why Too Much Medicine Is Making Us Sicker and Poorer (2007), you will remember that there are many things medicine is willing to treat that really don't respond to treatment. A person should have the nerve to say, "You don't know what's causing my problem and you don't know what will solve it; so why would I take that drug?" Doctors who treat migraine headaches seem to have reached the amazing conclusion that migraine headaches reflect *a narcotic deficiency in the patient*; the doctor is not paying any attention to the fact that the patient only gets that headache when she eats chocolate or when she drinks red wine the week before her period.

I heard Andrew Weil discussing migraines (Eating Well for Optimum Health, 2000). After the meeting, I asked him, "You mentioned that you think red wine and chocolate are *triggers* of migraines. Could you tell me the difference between a *trigger* and a *cause*?" He paused for a moment and said, "Well, I never really thought about it." What?!?!? He was willing to say that there is a connection or a relationship between these items and migraines but hadn't considered that they might actually *cause* the migraine! Folks, if red wine gives you a bad headache, don't drink it.

I really don't get this. All of conventional or traditional medicine treats *symptoms*. I think we discussed Aunt Emma and her bum knee earlier. Here is another classic example about how adrenalin is a reflection of the model of what medicine calls "phantom pain." The service man comes back from the war and his arm has been blown off. Whenever he gets allergic, or tired, or stressed, the missing hand hurts (thus, "phantom" as there is no hand). Another part of the brain sends out protective signals that cause the release of histamine (i.e., redness and swelling), and the muscles at the end of the arm contract strongly as the brain tries to hold the painful hand in a better position. This muscle "guarding" results in even more pain. I think that is what happens in the cases of fibromyalgia and arthritis. This is the same thing that happens to arthritis sufferers when their hands start to hurt. They have joints in their hands worn from 40 or 50 years of hand use. When they can't make cortisol, they will start putting out adrenalin. The doctor sees that and responds to his training. He first gives the patient cortisol (prednisone's the nasty drug used by many doctors who realize you are low on cortisol). Oral steroids have the most horrendous effects you can imagine. If we put somebody on oral steroids for a year, most would have irreversible side effects. Check out "oral steroids side effects prednisone" on Google and you will be convinced. Even six months could cause serious side effects. Oral steroids are not the answer. We know all our patients are low on cortisol (!!!!); what a handy solution that would be! The cortisol mechanism in the adrenal glands is so sensitive to feedback that if we add cortisol for very long, the adrenals won't make any. Now, we have a real problem. Now, we will have to supplement that cortisol forever and that is not easy to do. There are serious side effects. Cortisol can be added briefly, in low doses; but, we must carefully monitor the patient. (See Safe Uses of Cortisol, Wm. Mac Jeffries, 2004). A better solution is to find out what is *causing* the problem and *block* that.

➢ STEROIDS AS A TREATMENT

Injected steroids are also a problem. Rheumatologists love to inject swollen arthritic joints with steroids; they will stick a needle in that joint and try to suppress the inflammation with steroids, which works until the steroid wears off. But what are they going to do with the phantom pain that accompanies the swelling? Like our situation with the service man, I have a vision of the rheumatologist dodging around the patient trying to inject the missing hand! And this is the same attitude that rheumatologists have taken since the specialty began. They think the problem is in the joint, missing or not. If you believe that, then you are going to inject Aunt Emma's knee three days before every rainstorm with a steroid, or even replace her joint . . . if she will let you and if she has adequate insurance. They are happy to do this but this is *not* a solution. Interestingly, rheumatologists readily explain that there is no known cause for rheumatoid arthritis and there is no known treatment. Then they offer a cocktail of three very serious poisons to treat it.

One of them is called Methotrexate. Methotrexate is a cancer cell poison. It stops rapid cell division by poisoning the cells. Hope is that it will kill the cancer cells before it kills the patient. They use this drug on rheumatoid arthritis patients for extended periods of time, even when they don't have symptoms. They will tell you that once you get rheumatoid arthritis, you have it for life, and you will have to stay on these medications. A second one they commonly use in this little triumvirate of poisons is called Plaquenil. Plaquenil is a cell retardant as well, and Plaquenil causes blindness in 20% of its users within one year, so they will have your vision checked every few months while you are taking it. The third one in the group is prednisone. Prednisone is the nastiest steroid that has ever come along; it was the first one back in 1953. Within two years, they knew that it was a dangerous drug, because the lawsuits came rolling in. Since then, we have three generations of steroids: prednisolone, methylprednisolone, dexamethasone, and betamethasone. Each one has undergone different modifications over the ensuing 30 years to try to avoid the lawsuits and get a lower inflammatory effect.

Is this the best we can do for arthritis? Three poisons that don't work well? Most doctors are still using prednisone! Yet we had bioidentical cortisol available at the same time! Why aren't they using the one thing that would help patients the most? Simply because there is no *profit* in cortisol; you can get a month's supply for $12. Obviously, the drug companies won't push cortisol. To this day, in pulmonary residencies and rheumatology, they are still recommending prednisone. Why in the world would a doctor use a 50-year-old medication that has terrible side effects for a problem that really is not going to be solved by the prednisone anyway? You have to ask them.

➢ ALTERNATIVE TREATMENT AND FATAL DISEASES

I approach the problem differently. First, get rid of patients' symptoms by addressing the *causes*, not the symptoms. Then balance the hormones and address the stresses that led to the problem in the first place. When the patients go back to the rheumatologist, they may report improvements. The patients say they are fine and that they have not had any joint pain in six months. The doctor says, "Great, you are probably in remission." The patients respond, "No, ever since I saw Dr. Roby, I have not had any pain." The doctor's response: "Roby? Oh my God, you don't want to do that. You have to take drugs I gave you. This disease progresses whether you have symptoms or not. You must keep taking the drugs." They tell the doctor what I told them: "When the pain comes back, then I might take the drugs; until then, I am not going to do it." At the Roby Institute, we try not to fix things that work.

My view is that if you do not have symptoms, you do not treat them. Medicine does not operate that way. They will keep treating patients long after the symptoms have even gone, because they think the patient is "just in remission." The pulmonology doctors are treating inflammation in the lungs, severe asthmatics, chronic obstructive lung disease, and all manner of things that result in shortness of breath, with drugs. If the drugs don't work, if you still have increasing symptoms of shortness of breath, you could end up with a diagnosis of a fatal disease like polymyositis or IPF. The diagnosis depends on the key symptom of shortness of breath. Another of the key diagnostic elements of IPF is the fact that the disorder did not respond to treatment with prednisone, presumably eliminating *allergy* and inflammation from the equation. Yet, we got an average of 65% improvement of shortness of breath in 87% of our patients by blocking their allergic reaction to their own hormone progesterone.

All of the patients in our paper on "Progesterone as a Bronchodilator" had been diagnosed with "severe asthma" and all were on nebulizer treatment daily. As it turned out, only four of the 16 actually had asthma. The other 12 patients were incorrectly diagnosed. However, they all had severe shortness of breath and wheezing. We have successfully treated the symptoms of shortness of breath in severe cases of polymyositis and idiopathic pulmonary fibrosis. The fact that these symptoms could be dramatically diminished in a matter of seconds simply supports the idea that the diagnosis might have been incorrect. This leads one to wonder how many cases of unsuccessfully treated asthma, polymyositis, and pulmonary fibrosis might also be incorrectly diagnosed? Might they also be due to progesterone-mediated inflammation?

The question is, why would the pulmonary professors still be teaching the residents to treat a lung disease with systemic oral prednisone, which is going to affect the entire body? It affects the ankles, feet, knees, hips, brain, shoulders, and hands. Why treat the entire body with a drug, if you only need it in the lungs? If I want to treat the lung problem, I should use a medication that only targets the lungs, even a steroid can be limited to the lungs. I could give them an inhaled steroid for the lungs and completely avoid the whole body exposure that occurs with injections or oral dosages. Prednisone came out in the middle of the last century and medical students are *still* being instructed to use if for lung and joint pain. No one looks for the underlying *causes*; instead, they treat the symptoms. Patients do not like this and that is why Complementary and Alternative Medicine has an ever-increasing market share of health care. This is making traditional medicine frantic.

I get information all the time from the American Medical Association (AMA) talking about the advantages of adding vitamins, minerals, and supplements to my practice and that we should think about associating ourselves with a chiropractor or with an acupuncturist. Medicine is trying all sorts of things in an attempt to increase their market share, but it is not working. They do not really believe in any of those alternatives and they are going to continue to treat patients' symptoms with poisons. Patients, on the other hand, are realizing that traditional medicine is limited. Traditional medicine's market share was over 60% in the 1960s; now it is below 50% and people are using alternative treatments more and more every day. In this country wc spend *billions* of dollars on food supplements and vitamins. People are simply trying to treat themselves. My practice is exploding and I hear that traditional medical practices are not. Complementary and Alternative Medicine is a hot topic primarily because we are successful at finding *causes* rather than just treating symptoms. The public is becoming more and more aware of these Complementary and Alternative solutions. Many people are using the Internet. At one point, if they entered "hormone allegy" (an earlier term for progesterone-mediated inflammation) into Google, the first 18 entries on the first two pages all came to my Web site. My practice is prominent in the results of this type of search. Twenty-five percent of all of our new patients come to us as a result of the Internet. They come from all over the world and all around the United States. Traditional medicine says this type of test and treatment cannot happen, it does not exist, I have made it all up, and if you feel better, "it is all in your imagination . . . it's all a placebo effect." My patients don't really care. If the pain goes away, they don't care how we did it, or if they are imagining it. If they can breathe more easily, they don't care why it is happening. It wouldn't matter to them if we did it through prayer, voodoo, or magic crystals; they don't care, they just want the pain gone, the breathing easier, and we do that. Medicine says there is nothing in the literature to support this. No, and there never will be if not one of them will try it. For $40 worth of materials, one thousand Mayo Clinic pulmonary patients could be screened to see if this relieved shortness of breath and we would know the answer 15 seconds after the test was placed under the patients' tongues.

➢ THE CURRENT BELIEF SYSTEM

Suppose doctors were mechanics. Suppose you take your car into a medical garage and tell the doctor mechanic it wasn't running right and had a terrible knock. He pulls out the dipstick and says, "Sorry, I can still see oil. This car is just fine." Well, I wouldn't hesitate to say that you would find a new medical mechanic. However, people will put up with that sort of silliness from their doctors year after year. Their car keeps running off the road, but the doctor says you are just imagining that. They tell patients this and it really makes them angry. For decades, women have been telling these doctors that it is their hormones and yet the doctors say it can't be. "Can't be? Are you not listening to me? Every month like clockwork on the 25th day of my cycle, all hell breaks loose and you are telling me . . . it cannot happen? Are you hearing what I am saying? Do you think I am lying? Stupid? Crazy?"

Or, how about this . . . "You have severe pain in your bladder and you are not responding to any of our medical treatment . . . Therefore, we are going to surgically remove your bladder." Or, "You have IPF and there is nothing more that can be done for you except a lung transplant. You will probably live less than one year." Are you going for this? What do you mean . . . "There is nothing more that can be done"? Have we tried everything? What about sublingual progesterone drops? Dangerous? According to the World Health Organization there has never been a serious reaction to a sublingual antigen dose. Besides, how much more dangerous can it get than . . . "You have less than one year to live"?

What is going on here? This problem lies in the beliefs of the doctors. There is a very powerful mindset in that group. As we mentioned in Chapter 1, if it is not in The Book (of medicine), it doesn't exist. I don't care how much evidence you think you have, it doesn't exist. These are bright boys and girls, but there is a flaw in the medical education system and in their thinking. They were selected for their ability to memorize material. You remember the pre-med students – they weren't notoriously bright. They were really good at memorizing the material . . . chemistry, biology, physics. Selected for memory because there is so much to learn in medical school . . . much in The Book. If you wanted bright, you should look at a "EE" (electrical engineer), or any engineer, or a graduate student, even a pre-law. But not a pre-med. They are selected for their ability to learn the material they are taught. In Chapter 1, we mentioned Robert Laughlin, a Nobel Prize winner, who calls it "reductionism." He points out how science may overlook the obvious because we are spending so much time learning more and more about less and less. This is the idea of not being able to see the forest for the trees. This system will spit out anybody who asks questions; they are diverted and sent somewhere else. You see this in all universities. You get a famous scientist, some Nobel Prize winner, and his assistants are restricted to doing exactly what he did. They, in turn, are teaching their graduate students to do what they do, and this "trench" just gets deeper and deeper and deeper. We lose all sight of anything new, different, or innovative. We learn more and more about less and less. Anybody that doesn't go along with the party line is out. This, however, is not what the universities and medical schools were intended to do. It is not a part of their mission statements, but it is really what happens more often than they would like to admit.

Chapter 5

Hormones: "Normal" Levels

It was only 100 years ago in this country that women had an average life expectancy in 1900 of age 47; at the time of Christ, it was in the mid-20's. In 1900 years, life expectancy went from the mid-20's to the mid-40's. During that period, our bodies had to adjust to this life cycle. In the last 100 years, however, life expectancy has jumped from age 47 to age 86 for females in this country. Our bodies are having a difficult time catching up with medicine's ability to keep us alive longer. One hundred years has not been enough time for Nature to make this adjustment in the life cycle. If Nature thinks that you are going to be dead by 47 (Nature does not recognize these wonderful increases in our life spans), then by the time you are 40, she is going to start shutting down your reproductive hormones; Nature does not want people who are about to die to raise children. There would be no one there to raise the children.

I was married by the time I was 20. My main motivation was a driving need to make babies. By the time I was 23, I was a very stressed out young attorney with a wife, two children, and a mortgage. My first job as a law clerk for the Texas Court of Criminal Appeals paid $3,600 a year. Making babies was *way down* on my list of priorities. Nature, thinking we were only going to live to about 40, gave us fast reproductive hormones when were teenagers. So we reproduced. Then we saw a fairly rapid decline in our sex hormones (drive) by our mid-20's. Then started the natural decline leading to old age and death. On average, about 47 in 1900.

When our sex hormones go down, our bodies will use all our hormone assets to keep us fertile as long as possible. But that means a less important hormone (cortisol) will go way down. Herein lies the problem: when cortisol goes down, the backup, emergency hormone, adrenalin, goes up. Way up! And here we are! Adrenalized with all the pain and fatigue that results.

I see little girls who are starting their reproductive years younger and younger. In the United States, puberty begins at around 13 to 14 years of age. Most of my patients started their periods at 12 or 13 and we have two little girls in my practice that started their periods at age 6. The earlier that females start their reproductive years, the earlier they are going to end them. A few thousand years ago, when a young girl had her first period, they married her to a young man and they started having a family. At the time of Christ, girls began menstruating about 10-12, got married, and had their first child a year later; breast-feeding would protect them from getting pregnant for two more years. Then, they'd have a second, third, and fourth child, go into a fairly rapid decline, and be dead by their mid- to late-20's.

➢ THE BASIC "7"

I have found there are seven basic hormones that cause the most problems my patients experience. They are detailed below.

- *DHEA (Dehydroepiandrosterone)*

DHEA is the basic building block our bodies use to make all our other hormones. Without it, nothing works. If it is low, it will be used on the most essential hormones first. It peaks at about age 22 and then goes down rapidly. So, if your DHEA is low, it will go first for our absolutely essential adrenalin, then estrogen, then progesterone, then testosterone, then cortisol, and finally thyroid. Doctors don't know much about this because it (DHEA) was considered a dangerous drug until 1997, when it was changed from Class II (most dangerous) to over-the-counter. This occurred when it was shown to the FDA that DHEA had been in widespread use in Europe as an over-the-counter supplement with no harmful side effects. It was the second most popular supplement there, second only to St. John's Wort (the "poor man's" antidepressant).

I routinely order blood levels and find almost all of my patients are in the lowest ranges of normal. My experience tells me I have to get them up to mid-ranges before they can get in hormone balance.

- *ADRENALIN*

The adrenal gland sits on top of the kidneys and secretes adrenalin in emergency situations. It is an extremely powerful hormone that energizes the body for maximum effectiveness in "fight or flight" situations. When adrenalin is released into the bloodstream, it provides the brain and muscles with the *rocket fuel* they need for whatever is confronting them at the moment. When the body is short on cortisol, it must rely on our back-up emergency hormone . . . *adrenalin* to deal with allergies, stress, and energy. This is not what adrenalin is designed for, and using it in this manner can cause all sorts of problems in a variety of systems in the body.

- *ESTROGEN*

Estrogen is a powerful female hormone that helps young girls become women and allows them to reproduce. It is the "feel good" hormone for women. It is highest for the first five to seven years after periods begin. Then, it starts down. There are "receptors" all over the body where estrogens attach and cause a variety of effects. When levels of estrogen in females fluctuate and fall, any number of negative effects can occur, many of these around their periods. Urinary tract infections, mood swings, memory problems, changes in skin conditions, hot flashes, and a host of other bodily disorders can occur as a result of low estrogen or an estrogen "imbalance."

- *PROGESTERONE*

Progesterone is one of the hormones in our bodies that stimulates and regulates various functions. Progesterone plays a role in maintaining pregnancy. The hormone is produced in the ovaries, the placenta (when a woman gets pregnant), and the adrenal glands. It helps prepare your body for conception and pregnancy and regulates the monthly menstrual cycle. It also plays a role in sexual desire. It is the one hormone that seems to cause the most common allergies in women. I published the paper "Hormone Allergy," in 2006, demonstrating its role as an allergen. When we block it, we relieve all manner of symptoms in women and in many cases . . . in men as well.

- *TESTOSTERONE*

Testosterone is a hormone that is secreted mainly in the testes of males and in the ovaries of females; the adrenal glands secret small amounts of testosterone. Although most people think that testosterone is only a male hormone and only affects their sex drive, it is also found in females and plays a significant role in their sex drive and general health and well-being. Males produce much more of this hormone than females, but females are considerably more sensitive to much smaller amounts. Energy and drive is another area where testosterone plays a significant role. Low levels of testosterone can cause fatigue, pain, loss of focus, and loss of short-term memory. Some research suggests that testosterone levels can contribute to a loss in thinking skills and maybe even contribute to Alzheimer's disease and dementia. It is an accepted fact that as we age, our testosterone levels decrease. Raising these levels has proven to reverse many of these conditions. Testosterone is one of the hormones that we often need to increase in treating our patients.

- *CORTISOL*

Cortisol comes from the adrenal gland (as does adrenalin). Cortisol is the hormone we use for allergy (it prevents allergies, blocks swelling, and combats inflammation, such as in arthritis). For energy, it gives you the smooth, steady drive you need to get through the ordinary activities of your day, and for stress, it is your FIRST response to deal with stress or emergency needs. If you don't make enough cortisol to deal with these things, your adrenal gland will supplement it with the serious emergency hormone . . . adrenalin. If you have low cortisol, you might become more allergic and your doctor might realize your problem and prescribe cortisol (in the dangerous form of prednisone). He will give you the same thing for asthma and arthritis. He knows these conditions indicate low cortisol, but he has no clue as to "why" you have low cortisol. So, he frequently treats the symptoms by prescribing the pharmaceutical form of cortisol . . . *prednisone*. This is like plugging your jammed computer into a 220V outlet, rather than "re-booting" it. You are NOT going to get a good result.

- *THYROID*

The thyroid gland is at the base of your neck and controls how the body burns energy. The thyroid hormones secreted by the thyroid gland affect the body's rate of metabolism and influence the function of other systems in the body. One of the most common problems related to the thyroid is weight gain, but many other symptoms (hair loss, depression, circulation problems, cold hands and feet, etc.) are indicators of an under-active or an over-active thyroid gland, or at least thyroid hormones that are out of balance.

Women experience hormone changes every month, even after a complete hysterectomy. Our bodies are programmed on a 28-day cycle. We are all on a lunar 28-day cycle. Even those who have no plumbing left notice that one week a month they feel a little more sluggish and a little more swollen. So, we not only address the daily fluctuations but also the monthly fluctuations. As we age, these fluctuations continue and sometimes increase. There cannot be an 80-year-old man that feels as good as he did at 18; it just cannot be. So, we know that as we get older, all the hormones diminish, and even though there are some vigorous centenarians around, they are not what they were at 20. Even if I double their hormones, they will still be in the bottom 10% of the "normal" range, but they feel a *lot better*.

➢ "NORMAL" RANGES

The "normal range" of value for hormones is huge. DHEA, for example, is considered "normal" if the value is anywhere between 35 and 430! And that's for women of all ages. So, you're normal at a level of 35 whether you're 19 or 90! That is too strange for words. Women's "normal" range for testosterone is 14–76. How do you think a 20-year-old newlywed might feel with a "normal" value of 14? Not as good as she might with a level of 76! But, at either value, her doctor would tell her the test indicated she was . . . "just fine." If you fall anywhere within this very broad range of normal, then you are "okay." The problem with this is that the "normal" range is way too broad to be meaningful. Medicine defines diseases in terms of "abnormal" findings. Traditional medical doctors are the best in the world at detecting and treating "diseases"; but, they define *disease* as being outside the range of "normal" and adjust it regularly. Normal is defined as the middle 90% of a quarter of a million lab samples. You are abnormal in the 5% above 95% and you are abnormal in the 5% below. Everything in between is *normal*.

This is a ridiculously broad definition of "normal." This is like a "pass-fail" system in school. Anywhere from 5 to 95 you pass, you are "normal." Anything less than 5 or over 95 is "failing" or "abnormal." That is just too bizarre for words! Yet, that is what traditional doctors will tell you, that you are "fine" when your hormones levels might fall anywhere within that range! Wherever your hormone levels are, in range of "normal," at age 40, you can be sure they were a lot higher in the same range of normal when you were 20. If someone comes to me, for example, with thyroid levels in the bottom 10% of the normal range and I *tripled* their levels, they are still going to be in the bottom third of the normal. But they are going to feel a lot better.

Why do they have that wide range of normal and who decides this range? Pathologists decide normal ranges. Ranges make sense because they want to identify people who have diseases. Certainly those patients in the "abnormal" ranges are likely to have serious disorders. But this rigid reliance on a number is going to cause us to miss many patients who have a minor disorder of less than a full-blown disease. As a result, patients frequently say to me, "How is it that you will prescribe for me when I am in the normal range of lab values and my doctor won't?" I say, "The reason for that is that your doctor is not a lawyer. I went to law school before medical school and there I learned to think. Your doctor was taught about "normal" values in medical school. It was made very clear to all medical students that it was proper to treat some for a disease when you had *evidence* of the disease. Abnormal lab values were the only evidence we could rely on. If one prescribes something for a patient who has normal values and something happens, the doctor might be held responsible." So, doctors are afraid that if they give you thyroid and you die, your family might sue them and they might lose all their money. They are afraid other doctors would shake their fingers and say, "You shouldn't have prescribed for somebody that was in the normal range." Many doctors carry this deeply held conviction with them every day of their lives. They will not treat anything that falls in the normal range. Many traditional physicians take issue with this broad range of normal. Many of us think the ranges are excessively broad.

➢ NORMAL AND OBESITY

If you are 400 pounds and yet all your thyroid values are "normal," I would change that. You are very likely going to have a heart attack or a stroke because of this weight problem. You sure as hell are not going to die from increased thyroid levels.

Dr. Paul Cutter was one of our professors in medical school at the University of Texas. He was retired from private practice and came to the medical school to share his lifetime of experience treating his patients. When lab values were "normal" but his evaluation of the patient indicated problems, he told us we should always remember, "You are treating the patient . . . NOT the lab values." It takes a lot of skill and judgment to evaluate a patient. If we don't have those qualities, then we might feel compelled to rigidly follow the obvious evidence . . . the lab values. I think we should use lab values to *assist* us in our treatment of patients, not to exclude patients and deny treatment.

If you are experiencing symptoms of low thyroid and you have low "normal" levels of thyroid hormone, let's raise the levels. They will still be in the "normal" range. Why don't we take it back in the other direction? That is the main thing we do with weight problems. I think most health problems are a natural result of diminishing hormone levels as we age. Reproductive hormones are going to go down as we get past our reproductive years, so why wouldn't thyroid be affected similarly?

➢ DIABETES

In this country, women think nothing about having children at age 25, 30, 35, and beyond. Nature responds to that by cutting off the reproductive hormones. If the reproductive hormones go down, then we will make less cortisol. Cortisol, as we have noted, is the hormone we use for energy, stress, and allergies. If we are low in reproductive hormones, and as a result low in cortisol, then the only way we can get through our day is with that emergency hormone from the adrenal gland, adrenalin. I think this is the root cause in most of the problems in the patients I see. Patients are highly adrenalized because their reproductive hormones are low. If they don't have enough cortisol, they start running on adrenalin. We see that if you run on adrenalin, the emergency hormone designed to get you out of life-threatening situations ("fight or flight"), this burst of energy will last about two hours. Adrenalin can only use sugar for fuel. Blood sugar will drop like a rock. This adrenalin release will occur about every two hours, every day, seven days a week. By the end of each day, they are going to be so exhausted they cannot move because of all of these adrenalin surges. Their blood sugar is going to be jerked up and down with each surge. This explains one of the oldest known autoimmune disorders, diabetes. If we are going through these huge blood sugar swings, the pancreas is going to go into overdrive trying to provide us with insulin. The overactive pancreas cells attract the attention of our hypersensitive immune system which "kills" them, and then we get diabetes. Twenty-five percent of all Americans are supposed to have antibodies for their own thyroid for the same reason, but if we have a hormone imbalance, if we have diminished sex hormones (and everybody does after about 20), then we are going to see weight gain as the most common effect.

➢ WEIGHT AND HORMONES

I grew up on a farm in South Dakota. For centuries farmers have used sure-fire methods for making farm animals fat . . . you neuter them, feed them grain (carbs), and don't let them move (crowded feed lots). Nature is neutering all of us as we approach 40 because we eat carbs and we don't exercise. Sometimes the surgeons help with the neutering. We see women who have had hysterectomies or tubal ligations. As a result, we lose the effects of the reproductive hormones. Anybody who has any question about the effect of reproductive hormones should visit a ninth-grade class in high school and watch the interaction of sex hormones as you see bodies in constant state of action and agitation with very few people overweight. Sex hormones are tremendously powerful and when they begin to go down, Nature gives us the only thing that is useful to a dying person, storage fat in the middle of the body. Anybody who has been around a farm has seen what happens to bulls that are neutered and chickens that are turned into capons. Any farm animal that we castrate is immediately going to start gaining weight in the middle of the body and they are not going to be sexually active. I do not know if they are depressed or not, but I can assure you that is what happens to many humans.

➢ REVERSE NEUTERING – CHANGE DIET

So, what we do is we put these hormones back, and we get the patients to stop eating the carbs that facilitate weight gain. What do we feed the cattle that will be most effective at making them fat? Carbohydrates. Grains and carbohydrates. Grains like corn, wheat, oats, and barley. We feed the pigs overripe fruit and carbohydrates because these are the things we have learned are most effective at putting fat on neutered animals.

So, my patients say, "Well, what can I eat?" The most important thing is to remember to avoid carbohydrates. I tell them, "We have balanced your hormones so that you are no longer a neutered farm animal; now, when you sit down to a meal you must ask yourself, 'Do I want to eat like a feed lot cow?'" The cows are going to eat the grains and this translates to many of your favorite things, like pizza, pasta, bread, cake, cookies, and cereal.

➢ MOVEMENT AND HORMONES

We have to move more. If Nature is turning us into old people, then we need to act more like young people. I want you to act more like you did when you were 30. That means more movement, more social activity, more sexual activity, and more spiritual activity. Spirituality is a health tool that we have had forever. Use all the tools at your disposal. If we do all of these things, there is a real good likelihood we may not need to go see a doctor. We may find out that the doctor is right, that we do not have any kind of disease . . . we have a hormone imbalance.

When I was 50, my wife looked me in the eye and said, "Is it me?" I told her it would not matter if she were a 20-year-old centerfold, there was nothing going on here . . . nothing. Then we measured my testosterone and it was the level of a very old man, way below the bottom range of normal. When I took testosterone, I got my level four times higher than it was and it was still below the range of normal. By adding even more testosterone, I am in the bottom 15th percentile for all aged men, and yet I am feeling a lot better than I did. This is what we run into every day in our office.

To some extent, doctors are frustrated because they do not know what to do about abnormal hormones. It wasn't something they were taught in medical school. When they see the 300-pound woman who has no sex drive, fatigue, and loss of short-term memory, they know the she has a problem. But what are they going to give her? Amphetamines! That is about all they know to do for a weight problem, because they are not prepared to treat hormone *imbalances*. They were not trained to deal with imbalances in the "normal" levels of hormones. They often don't even know how to order the hormone tests.

➢ MEDICINE – LEARNING MORE ABOUT LESS

Medical Science is learning more and more about less and less. Did you know that we have doctors for the front of the eye? Corneal specialists. For the back of the eye? Retina specialists. I see pain patients who have been to six different specialists. They have been to an internist or family practice doctor for the pain. They couldn't find anything wrong so they referred them to a neurologist. The neurologist tells them they may have something wrong but he can't tell what it is, what causes it, or what will help it. Along with the pain, they have severe indigestion and chest pain, so they are referred to a gastroenterologist and a cardiologist who say they have GERD and some tachycardia (rapid heartbeat). This indicates allergy to me, resulting in an acid stomach and rapid heart rate due to the adrenalin we secrete when we have allergies. The allergy and adrenalin can lead to an acid stomach and irritable bowel syndrome (IBS) . . . a stomachache. The belly pain may lead them to an OB/GYN who says they have endometriosis with "no known cause and no known treatment." The joint pain leads them to the rheumatologist who says he has no idea why their pain is moving from joint to joint but there is "no known cause and no known treatment." All the specialists tell the patient there is nothing wrong with them. The psychiatrist tells them they are emotionally upset and they probably need an antidepressant. The problem with all this is that these doctors do not talk to one another. All the doctors will agree on one thing . . . there is way too much wrong with this person for not having any kind of a disease. So the doctors naturally enough conclude the patient is nuts and they try to shut them up. With chemicals. With antidepressants.

From time to time, patients will tell me all the normal values their doctor reported. And I say, "Wait, wait. Your doctor is wrong and that is why you are here." Nobody comes to see me to tell me how successful their treatment has been . . . how great they feel. About once a year someone will come into my office who is really sick. They ask me what I think they should do and I tell them I think they should see their traditional doctor. If they are bad enough I might suggest calling 911 and we can have an ambulance come pick them up and take them to the emergency room. I do not treat sick people. Traditional doctors do that. Really well. On the other hand, those traditional doctors are not very good at treating people who are not *sick*, but still suffer with pain or other symptoms. There is a difference between being sick with a disease and simply *feeling* sick.

When I was a little kid, my mother read me fairy tales. One was about a king in Africa who heard of another king in the next country who had a strange animal and he wanted to hear more about it. So, he sent his six Wise Men to examine this animal, called an elephant. The Wise Men came back and each one gave him a different report; one of them said the elephant was a tall hose going up to the sky. Another said it was big and flat with hair on it. Each one gave a different report. Well, it turned out the Wise Men were all blind and they did not talk to one another. That is what we see in medicine today. We have all these wise men who do not talk to one another. They are all examining pieces of the puzzle but nobody steps back to see it is an elephant. They are blinded by their limited knowledge, limited to their specialty.

Rarely do I see a patient in the *high* range of normal. I rarely see that because these people with high levels of hormones usually don't have health problems. The patients I see almost always have low normal or out-of-range low levels of one or more hormones. If they have one, two, or three hormones that are in the lowest range of normal with the rest in the upper ranges, this may result in a huge imbalance. All I have to do is balance the hormones, get the low ones closer to others and then they may not be forced to use adrenalin for all their daily activities. If even one hormone is out of balance, the body may go straight to adrenalin. We need balanced hormones to avoid adrenalin surges and all the symptoms that they can cause.

Chapter 6

Hormones: Bioidenticals, Allergies, and "Neutralization"

Bioidentical hormones are compounds that have exactly the same chemical and molecular structure as hormones that are produced in the human body. Though any hormone can be made to be "bioidentical," the term is often used to describe formulations containing estrogens, progesterone, and testosterone. Bioidentical hormones are made from natural substances, and they are designed to exactly copy the hormones that the body makes and the effects they have on the body. These compounds are fairly new. I have been prescribing them for the last 15 years. The reason I prefer these bioidentical hormones is straightforward. Pharmaceutical companies cannot patent a natural hormone, so the only way they can patent and market it is to add some type of a "side-chain" to it; they have to make it unique somehow, but this also makes it different than the naturally occurring hormone the body makes. There has never been any profit available from making an exact copy of a body hormone, since they cannot patent it, so they make similar copies, counterfeit copies of the real thing.

However, in the last several years, technology has advanced to the point where we can crank a chemical formula into a machine and it will turn out drugs at the other end matching any chemical formula we enter. As a result, pharmacies, known as "compounding pharmacies," are able to use natural substances (yams, for example) and make hormones that are bioidentical to the ones that the body makes, which in our view will cause minimal, if any, side effects. Additionally, they can make a profit on each of these compounds and still offer them at a price lower than many pharmaceutical products such as Premarin and Provera, the pharmaceutical counterfeits of body hormones. As a result, we prescribe bioidentical hormones for women where it is necessary to add one or more for supplement or replacement. We usually do not have to prescribe hormones for younger women. If a woman is under 30, there is a really good possibility that all we might have to do is block some of her progesterone-mediated inflammation and her body will resume the natural production of hormones on its own. Their bodies will resume natural hormone production when we block the progesterone-mediated inflammation and relieve the stress that is initially causing the imbalances.

Hormone replacement therapy (HRT) or supplementation becomes much more significant and common in women over 40. It gets critical in women over 50. This is also necessary in men where we often use testosterone supplements; there is not a man on Earth that has the same levels of testosterone at 60 as he had at 20. Doctors are becoming more and more involved in replacing hormones in men and women. Complementary and Alternative doctors are most likely to prescribe supplements we refer to as bioidentical hormones. We also pay attention to vitamins, minerals, and supplements that might be low.

In my own case, I did a vitamin and mineral study. It came back indicating very low levels of vitamin B12 and folate. We cannot eat vitamin B12, our body has to make it, or we have to inject it. When I began vitamin B12 injections, I felt dramatically better. We test to determine what the patient might be reacting to or be deficient in. We use this information to suggest vitamins, minerals, or other supplements that might help the patients achieve a better balance. This often involves hormones, but it is *always* going to involve dietary changes and it *must* involve an increase in their movement. I choose not to refer to movement as "exercise" because many people have fairly negative feelings about exercise. However, we do want the patients to *move* more.

➢ PROGESTERONE–MEDIATED INFLAMMATION

We have tested patients with many different substances over the years. The progesterone reaction causes adrenalin surges and this leads to all kinds of symptoms, pain being the most common. In four cases out of five, women are going to feel better if we block their reaction to progesterone. We also block estrogen. This has led us to seek and receive a patent for the use of progesterone in the sublingual drop form to combat a wide variety of disorders, some of which were thought to be fatal diseases. All of these things that have to do with adrenalin can be addressed by blocking the progesterone reaction, i.e., blocking the *progesterone-mediated inflammation*.

Some people are allergic to their own hormones, which falsely lowers their hormone levels. The paper I published on this topic, "Hormone Allergy," has been widely disregarded by traditional physicians. It was published in The American Journal of Reproductive Immunology in 2006. In it we demonstrate IgE antibodies to hormones progesterone and estrogen. This is Type I Allergy. Progesterone-mediated inflammation patients are those who have issues that are clearly related to hormones: premenstrual asthma, premenstrual migraine, interstitial cystitis, vulvodynia, and fibromyalgia. Any disorder that gets worse each month before or after a period begins is probably related to an allergic reaction to your own hormones, usually progesterone, but sometimes estrogen. I have never, in 30 years, run into a woman who did not realize that her symptoms, whatever they were, had some connection to her hormones. Women are conditioned to being aware of their bodies from the time they start menstruating. There is a 28-day cycle and they are acutely aware of the changes each month. Men do not go through that. Males are more difficult to treat. All guys were raised with the idea that if there is not bright, red blood running out of their pant leg, they are "okay." Girls, on the other hand, are aware of their cycles. They know when they are "on" and they know when they are "off." So, most women are aware of their hormones, only to go and have their doctor look over his glasses and say, "That's not possible. That doesn't happen." After awhile, the patient begins to believe the doctor. "Maybe it's not happening, maybe I'm losing my mind, maybe I'm imagining it, maybe it is 'all in my head.'" To which we reply, "Of course it is . . . all in your head." After all, that's where your brain is and that is where the adrenalin is having its effect. That is where the problem is located . . . in your head. Just because he cannot find it, does not mean you do not have it.

➢ NEUTRALIZATION

All of this work began with my studies at the Pan American Allergy Society, a group of ear, nose, and throat (ENT) doctors who believed in immediate desensitization through the use of shots. Starting in 1939 and continuing today, many ENT allergists use allergy injections of very weak strength. Traditional allergists use much stronger doses and as a result, the shots that they give people frequently cause serious side effects, sometimes even anaphylaxis (severe allergic reactions, even death). Pan American Allergists and homeopathy physicians will use amazingly weak doses from one tenth to one millionth as strong as the doses used by traditional allergists. Traditional medicine has a very difficult time with this, because from a chemist's point of view, if you weaken something enough, you eventually get to the point where there is nothing left in the drops. Yet, we know that these drops still have an impact on patients. In fact, we can demonstrate that they do. We have patients who can get dramatically worse on the weakest dilutions possible we give them. The patients have no idea what is in the drops, so the fact that we can make their symptoms better or worse, depending on the strength of the drops, clearly demonstrates that the patients are having allergic reactions to the drops. We have found that much stronger dilutions give us the same kind of relief and it is much longer lasting.

Back in Chapter 2, we discussed how we use sublingual drops to produce the same effect as an allergy injection in a patient, with none of the discomfort. We also talked about the speed of sublingual drops, relieving symptoms in just a few seconds. The drops that I have tried over the years started out with the common things I learned in Pan American Allergy Society training courses, which were basically pollens and molds. But in 1976, I was practicing in Carmel, California, and a lady came in who had a 10 (on a scale from 1 to 10) itch across the bridge of her nose. She had a deep red rash that spread from one cheek to the other and it itched so intensely that she was frantic; this had been going on for three years and nobody had been able to do anything about the itching rash on her nose. She had been to dermatologists with no relief. If she kept large amounts of steroid cream on the rash, it diminished the intensity but this had affected her skin as well. As soon as she stopped using the steroid cream, the itching would come back with a vengeance. Nothing had made that itch better in three years. The rash was very prominent when I saw her and she was itching at what she described as a 10 level. In her information sheet, she had listed her place of work as the Nestle Chocolate Factory in Salinas, California. Since I was getting no response whatsoever from pollen and mold (which we really would not expect as they do not usually show up as skin rashes), it had occurred to me that the rash might have something to do with chocolate. On her next visit, I had her bring a little packet of Nestles chocolate powder with her and we mixed it in water and made a very weak solution. I INJECTED it under her skin, which is the way we tested people in those days, and in front of our eyes, the redness began to disappear. It got better and better and she was quite shocked because within a few moments, she said the itching had completely disappeared, for the first time in three years!

In those days, my associate, Dr. Mark Snellen, and I had conducted mold studies that we published in the Annals of Allergy, Asthma and Immunology. I sent Dr. Snellen to a local camera store, where he rented a Kodak movie camera. He brought it back and filmed the reaction to show the color changes in the rash. We found we could make the woman's rash *come and go* in about 30 seconds by using stronger or weaker solutions of the chocolate. I showed that film in meetings for years and years. Unfortunately, in all the moves I have made, I have lost the film, but the lesson was never lost on me. If we find out what the patient is reacting to and use a dilution of it, we can diminish the symptoms. If we use a strong concentration of it, we can bring the symptoms back, and weaker makes the symptoms disappear. Allergists typically use airborne antigens like pollen and mold, but more and more we use other substances like hormones, to block symptoms of all types, chiefly pain. In the last 50 years, it became more and more clear that injecting the materials under a patient's skin could be dangerous; this can cause some serious reactions, even death. This is why most allergists required patients to get their allergy shots in the doctors' offices. After the shot, the patient should remain there up to two hours to make sure they don't have a dangerous reaction. All of the international literature was indicating that sublingual testing or treatment was becoming more and more popular in Europe, particularly in Great Britain where it has been the only means of treating allergy for the last 10 years. They have not done injections since the late 90's. A paper published by the World Health Organization indicates that sublingual desensitization, which has been in the literature since the early 1960's, has *never* caused a single serious reaction, so we know it is a very safe method to use. We can use almost any kind of an antigen sublingually and we have no reason to expect a bad result, because there has never been a single case of *anaphylaxis* due to sublingual testing or treatment.

Anaphylaxis is an immediate hypersensitivity reaction that shuts down the body and can cause cardiac arrest, pulmonary arrest, even death. Obviously, we want to avoid reactions of this kind, so we stopped doing injections and began to test and treat almost everybody sublingually by the mid 1990's, and when we tested people, we would try to test them for the things to which we suspected they were allergic. For example, if someone comes in and tells me they have seasonal allergies, we test them for pollens and molds and treat them accordingly. If they have terrible reactions in the fall, depending on where they live, we know it is ragweed; if they have terrible reactions in the middle of the winter, we know it is Mountain Cedar in Texas, pine trees in Colorado, and other trees in other areas; and if they have terrible symptoms in the spring we test for flowers and trees or in the summer for grass. We test for those things and, depending on what season it is and what the patient might be reacting to, we would pretty well be able to effectively treat their symptoms.

➢ NEUTRALIZATION AND ALLERGIES

More and more women had complained to me over the years about the fact that they thought they were having some kind of reaction to their hormones. For 30 years, women have been telling me that they are certain something is going on with their hormones and there is a considerable body of medical literature having to do with hormone related disorders. Premenstrual asthma and premenstrual migraine have been described in the literature for over 50 years. These are *clearly* related to hormones, and yet traditional medicine has always maintained that no allergic reaction could have anything to do with hormones because hormone molecules are too small. Molecules this small are called *haptens* and by definition they are too small to cause an allergic reaction. But penicillin is a hapten also and we know it can cause allergy. Consequently, in the paper mentioned earlier, we demonstrated progesterone-mediated inflammation by showing how the tiny molecules were *linked* to larger protein particles which *are* capable of causing allergic reactions and that the hormone determines the identity of the particle. We demonstrated that patients can be allergic to their own hormones and we began to test them by trying to use weak amounts of the very hormones we suspected they were allergic to; this has led to dramatic success in diminishing all manner of symptoms, but in particular pain, premenstrual asthma, and premenstrual migraine.

In our discussion of neutralization, which is on our Web site (www.robyinstitute.com), you will see the statistics on over 450 patients tested for 12 different categories of pain and discomfort. Across the board, we see about 65% reduction of all symptoms in about 75% of all patients, and that was simply by blocking their symptoms with sublingual drops of weak solutions of progesterone. We made videotapes of these patients showing their responses to sublingual progesterone drops. Since then we have had special software designed that allows us to enter the VAS symptoms and scores of patients are screened with sublingual drops. We only record patients who have symptoms severe enough to register 7 or higher on our scale of 0 to 10 with 10 being the worst symptoms they have experienced. We have nearly 1,000 patients entered in this database recording their changes in various symptoms in response to the drops. The software allows us to see what percentage of relief of any type of symptom is achieved with various drops. The numbers are all proving to be consistent with our first studies.

Of all the different things that we have tested (pollens, molds, viruses, bacteria, luteinizing hormones, follicle stimulating hormones, estrogen, testosterone, and progesterone), the one that uniformly resulted in the greatest reduction in symptoms is progesterone. As a result, we focus much of our testing and treatment on symptoms we can relieve with progesterone. If that does not relieve *all* their symptoms, during this initial visit, then we will try some other hormones as well as pollens and molds. Typically, those who are going to react best to progesterone are the women who started their periods before 13, who have an increase in symptoms the week before their period (when their progesterone is highest), and who get better as soon as their period begins. We will relieve those symptoms with progesterone, regardless of the time of their cycle, although the relief will be more dramatic at a time when they are most reactive, which is when they ovulate and the week before their period. On the other hand, if their symptoms get worse when they begin their period, then we have to suspect that they are reacting to the hormone estrogen. If, after our initial test with progesterone the patient still has some symptoms left, then we will move on and test further with estrogen to see if we can further diminish their symptoms, our objective being to reduce all their symptoms, if possible.

➢ NEUTRALIZATION: THE PROCESS

We have had our own software designed so that every time a new patient comes in, we enter their symptoms. First, we find out what their symptoms are and then get patients to evaluate those symptoms on a system of responses and calculate the percent improvement in each symptom in response to each set of drops – 0 to 10 with 10 being the worst they have felt with those symptoms and 0 being no symptoms. This is known as a Visual Analog System (VAS) and it is considered to be acceptable scientific evidence. When the patients come in, they assign a number to their symptoms and then we start out by putting a placebo under their tongue. We just use a blank dose of water and see if they can feel any difference and of course, as one would expect in any patient population, about 10% to 20% will feel some difference from the placebo drops. This is called the "placebo effect," a common phenomenon in scientific studies. Then we move on to the airborne antigens and our first test will be with the seasonal antigen that is in the air. We again check all their symptoms in any categories they have identified. We have the patients reevaluate their symptoms after each set of drops. As the symptoms range, the patient notes those changes in the VAS system; then we try the next substance, a series of progesterone drops.

We have found that if we use a weak dilution of progesterone, immediately followed by a stronger dilution, followed by the strongest dilution, this sets up the best possibility for reducing symptoms. If there are any symptoms left (of 3 or greater), then we will try a single estrogen test. If there are still symptoms left, we might try a virus. Finally, particularly in cases of sinusitis or sinusitis pressure, we would try a dilution of bacteria. By this time, most of our patients have seen a dramatic reduction in most of their symptoms. This allows us to explain to the patient what might be causing their symptoms. If it is airborne things, pollens and molds, then we can recommend traditional treatment through a visit to their allergist or desensitization with pollens and molds, antihistamines, and supportive therapy. If we find out that they are reacting to their own hormones, then we are going to suggest a blood test to determine the hormone so we can try to figure out how to put the hormones in better balance. This is particularly significant in females over 40.

I treat more women than men, by a ratio of about 9 to 1. Men don't often come in complaining about their "hormone problems." If a guy is in pain and he does not notice it, does he really have a problem? Probably not . . . certainly not one that he needs addressed. There has to be a *really* serious problem before a guy is going to go to the doctor. Only a few things will get him to make that call. Things like a heart attack, a broken bone, or ED (erectile dysfunction) will probably do it, but that's about it. I have always maintained that if a guy comes into my office with an oxygen bottle under his arm and a plastic tube snaking up to his nose, he is going to do whatever I tell him to do . . . just long enough to get rid of that oxygen bottle and swing his golf clubs again. But as soon as that happens, he is through, he is gone, and he is smoking cigars and drinking that beer, just as he always did. Guys are very straight-line thinkers. If he cannot breathe without an oxygen bottle, if it is interfering with his golf swing, he will come in. Guys do not pay attention to their health . . . women do. Women are used to watching monthly that ebb and flow. They can tell you fairly precisely which day of the cycle the problems begin. And it tends to happen to all of them in the same house, at the same time. Woe to the man with four teenage daughters and a wife because all of them are likely to react at the same time; this is why men invented hunting season, fishing season, and golf trips; they are going to have to leave home. I think they used to board up sorority houses for one week a month.

➢ ALLERGY – HOW DID WE GET HERE?

From the beginning of time, allergy was a "lethal gene," a deadly genetic trait. Allergy is caused by low levels of cortisol. If we have low levels of cortisol, we will become allergic. If we are allergic we will get the side effects of allergy . . . excessive mucus and soft tissue swelling. This often leads to throat infections, sinus infections, and respiratory infections.

These infections were usually fatal diseases of childhood, until about 1941. I was remarkably allergic and "sickly" as a child and young adult. My allergies cleared up when I reached puberty, and I was pretty healthy until I ran into a bunch of stress as an intern when I was 32 years old. My daughter and son have much more dramatic allergies than I do, and my grandchildren have greater allergies than their parents do. The trait increases from generation to generation, which is why we are seeing more and more people with allergies. This also explains why doctors are more and more mystified by all these strange symptoms. This was not covered in any of the stuff I was taught in medical school. *Nobody mentioned allergy*. There was not one lecture on it and there was no reference to it, except for that comment about the occasional anaphylactic reaction to foods. There was a lot of information on immunology and the autoimmune diseases, but little was said about ordinary allergy and the symptoms it could cause. I started medical school in 1969 and there was an allergist/ immunologist on the faculty, but there was no board certification and there was no residency for allergists at that time. In fact, the field of allergy only goes back about 100 years. Symptoms we used to think were caused by a "cold" or "virus" are now recognized as the symptoms of allergy: sniffles, sneezes, red eyes, and nasal congestion.

Allergy (food or airborne) causes an increased secretion of mucus from the turbinates that are located in the back of the nasal passages. These turbinates are loaded with mucus and they are designed, by God, to provide mucus for lubrication for our food. These large sacs of mucus that hang in the upper part of the back of the nose are like teats on a cow, and when we squeeze them as we chew, they bring down mucus that is supposed to coat the food. The food coated with mucus then slides down the esophagus into the stomach, where the mucus must be resistant to the action of stomach acid. It cannot be broken down by hydrochloric acid, or it would serve no purpose below the stomach. Yet we know that the mucus has to lubricate the GI tract all the way down to the rectum; we reabsorb the mucus in the last third of the intestinal tract, particularly in the colon.

Anybody who has raised children realizes that when the infant has diarrhea, mucus appears in the diaper, mixed with the stool, because the transit time of the material through the child's gut has been so fast that there was not enough time to reabsorb the mucus. So, mucus from the nose coats the food. Chewing moves the soft palate up and down and this "milks" mucus out of the turbinates. This mucus coats the food and acts as a lubricant all the way down the gut. But, the mucus is made of a *buffered* protein. It is important to realize that this causes the stomach to put out enormous amounts of acid, in order to dissolve the protein. But the mucus is buffered, which means it cannot be broken down by the acid. So, here we have a substance the stomach treats just like a hamburger. Well, the allergic person has turbinates that swell and become more and more full. We swallow mucus constantly. If we didn't, our throats would turn to dust. But allergy patients secrete and swallow much more than ordinary folks. Allergy patients are constantly clearing their throats. This is from mucus that is going down the back of their throats in meal-size quantities. The stomach thinks the person is eating a meal of mucus "hamburger" and secretes enormous amounts of acid, trying to dissolve it.

Many of my allergy patients have something that the gastroenterologists refer to as gastroesophageal reflux disease (GERD); and they do, but that simply describes the symptoms. It does not address the cause. The cause is the acid build up in the stomach in response to all the SNOT! If we swallow large amounts of mucus, we are going to have an acid stomach. So, should we take an H2 blocker like Prilosec or Prevacid, a "purple pill," or should we cut off the mucus, so that we stop the *cause* of the acid? Medicine, using its straight-line method of problem solving, will attempt to block the acid itself, so doctors give you antacids. They give you H2 blockers. They have all manner of chemicals designed to give symptomatic relief for the acid, but nobody pays any attention to the fact that the patient is sitting there snuffling and gagging on copious amounts of mucus drainage. If we can dry up the patient's nose, stop the mucus flow, then we do not have a problem with the stomach. The mainstay of the treatment of allergy (and many stomach issues) in our office is to "dry up" the nose.

➢ FOOD SENSITIVITY

This leads us to the question of why we ask all of our patients, regardless of the symptoms, to pay attention to food. I ask all my new patients to restrict certain food groups for a period of five days. All the things we treat, pain, shortness of breath, weight problems, fatigue, loss of short-term memory, low sex drive, whatever . . . is almost always affected by food. Whether we are allergic or have any of the other problems, one of the factors is always . . . adrenalin. Adrenalin causes pH changes in the stomach. It becomes more and more acidotic and starts reacting to foods that would not normally cause us any problems. For example, let's say the acid in the stomach is "medium" under normal conditions. If we drink milk at that point, then that "medium" acid, that normal acid level, would cause the MILK to be broken down into two parts: let's say, for the sake of discussion, MI and LK. Those parts would then pass down into the rest of the intestinal tract, where we have our most sensitive allergy "defender" cells to protect us in the case of poison, or virus, or bacteria that might post the deadly acid bath in the stomach. The acid bath in the stomach is supposed to destroy virus, bacteria, and poisons, but if any of them get by, then we have one last line of defense that causes an immediate reaction. These defender cells in the gut will grab anything that looks dangerous and attach itself to it. This new "antigen-antibody" unit is so heavy it moves out into the blood stream where the "enemy" can be attacked and destroyed by the white blood cells and other components of our immune system.

When pH (a measure of acid strength) changes in the stomach because of mucus drainage, we have a *very* acidic stomach. If we are swallowing large amounts of mucus, the stomach can become acidic so that, if we were to drop a block of *wood* into it, the block would be dissolved in a vapor of gas. This is a comment I hear frequently from patients: "When I eat, I feel that I am gassy, I burp and get cramps, and an upset stomach." That happens because of powerful acid increasing because of the mucus when the acid in this strong food is broken down into unusual fragments. MILK, instead of being broken down into MI and LK, may be broken down into MIL and K. The cleavage point in the protein chains changes with the changing acidity of the stomach, so that now we get a huge number of unique fragments. When those pass down into the intestines, the defender cells look at them and say, "This doesn't look right. Let's attack it. This might be poison. Kill it!" As a result, we have swelling in the gut. The process of moving food slowly through its intestines is slowed or stopped or speeded up. The result is either rapid intestinal flow (diarrhea) or, more likely, stopped intestinal movement which results in constipation. If we have swelling in an area where a reaction takes place, where defender cells are grabbing weird food fragments, no movement takes place past that area.

As a result, we see patients who feel terribly blocked up as a result of food reactions. This does not happen in an ordinary person, somebody who does not have a hypersensitive gut and who does not swallow lots of mucus. When they drink milk and it is not broken down into precise parts like MI and LK, their gut doesn't pay any attention. They do not have a supersensitive allergic gut and so it lets MIL and KM pass saying, "Well, that's close enough. Let's not worry about it." But in people with allergies, their gut has a very sensitive mechanism that is easily tripped by anything that is not *exactly* right. Consequently, these patients' guts think they are being poisoned on a regular basis and the gut reacts and swelling is the result. Sometimes, if that happens in the stomach, they will have stomach pain after a meal or stomach discomfort. The level of discomfort indicates which foods you are hypersensitive to and how sensitive you are. Some people react to a food in a hypersensitive fashion when the mere odor of the food reaches them. For example, some people get terribly itchy red eyes or their eyes might swell completely shut when someone cuts an onion in their presence. They may have an itchy severe burning of their nose just from the vapor of the cut onion in the air. This makes it pretty easy for them to tell what did it. They *know* that cut onions cause their allergic symptoms. If your lips swell three or four times their usual size whenever a particular food or drink touches them, then it becomes easy to tell what is causing the reaction. I have patients whose tongues swell. I have one patient whose tongue would swell right out of his mouth whenever he drank a certain soft drink. It looked like an avocado; it was so large he could barely breathe. We wondered how it took him so long to discover that every time he drank the soft drink, his tongue swelled. He even brought a video showing the reaction. He wanted me to test him and find out which chemical in the drink was causing the reaction. I told him to just stop drinking it.

➢ FOOD ALLERGY

We are all very slow to learn these things. For some reason, we crave the very things to which we react, to which we are allergic. More common than tongue swelling is throat swelling. Some people get an itching and swelling in their throat when they eat a particular kind of food. Most common is stomach discomfort. When we eat a food, one to five minutes later we start having stomach cramps and discomfort. Sometimes it can be so severe that the food will just come right back up. If it happens that fast, then it is pretty easy for the patient to know which food is causing the problem. Then that is very clear and that patient does not eat that food, I hope. It gets a little more dicey when the reaction is in the intestines, below the stomach, because that is over an hour after we ate the food. I react immediately to orange juice, the minute I taste it my tongue is on fire. My tongue also burns if I eat jalapeño peppers, and I mean burns a *lot more* than the ordinary jalapeño pepper eater's tongue. My tongue burns so badly that I feel like I have to immerse my head in cold water to get rid of it. But most of my reactions are in my stomach and those can be reversed with a food "antidote." (One of the best food reaction antidotes is magnesium. One can also use Alka–Seltzer or club soda to neutralize these reactions or even baking soda.)

I also react lower down in my intestines. That occurs one to three hours after I eat apples. If I eat bread, in four or five hours, I am going to have this amazing feeling of "fullness" in my lower belly, which strangely enough, makes me think if I ate *more* bread, the discomfort would be relieved. I have learned from painful experience that that is not the case at all and nothing good will result. I will continue to swell and bloat until the blockage is relieved by a bowel movement. I have many patients who tell me the only time they feel good is after a bowel movement.

➢ CONSTIPATION

Constipation is quite common among my patients. Therefore, we try to promote regular and frequent bowel movements to keep these foods moving. Some only have movements twice a week. I once did. We try to help the patient identify which foods are causing the problem and avoid those foods. We want them to have twice-a-day, formed stools and we will go to some lengths to achieve this. The more we react to foods, the less often we go to the bathroom. I even have patients that go *once* a week. Until we correct this, it can lead to all sorts of medical problems. If you are even more unlucky, you might react in the very last parts of the intestines. If you react lower down in your bowel, that might be a food you ate one or two days earlier. If this is the case, it is very hard to tell what caused it. Even more problematic is someone whose bottom breaks out in a rectal rash when the food comes out; that could be food eaten two or three days earlier. However, the most difficult situations of all are the skin problems. The dermatologists freely admit that atopic dermatitis, eczema, and psoriasis have something to do with food, but they do not know what. The problem is that people who have skin conditions are indeed reacting to foods. But it is a food they ate up to *30 days* before. The toxins move very slowly up through the layers of the skin. It takes the skin about 30 days to replace the surface cells with the base cells, and if it is that long since you ate the food, there is no way to tell which food (or foods) is causing the reaction. These patients have a particularly difficult path in that they must restrict their foods for several weeks at a time before we see any improvement in their condition.

Food sensitivity occurs then when we are suffering from our seasonal airborne allergies. It only happens when there is a pH or acid change in the stomach because we are swallowing mucus as a result of the airborne allergy.

For example, I am terribly allergic to Mountain Cedar, which in Austin, Texas is a season that runs from Thanksgiving to the middle of February. During that time, I have to be particularly careful about everything I eat because it is quite likely I will react. Food reactions make me stupid, inducing a loss of short-term memory and causing a deep depression. During my allergy "season" (I have three), I have to eat *very*, *very* carefully. I can only eat organic chicken or fish that is prepared with no seasoning except salt. I can only eat cooked vegetables and I can only drink bottled water. If I eat *anything* else, there is a good likelihood I am going to become terribly sick and feel much worse than I did had I not eaten at all. In fact, all my life I have realized that I feel best when I do not eat. I have "fasted" off and on since my teenage years. Well, we cannot "not" eat for very long, and as a result, most of us have to be terribly careful to avoid food reactions during our allergy season.

True food allergy is rare. These are people who have a Type I allergic reaction to a food. Type I is an *immediate* reaction. These are people who have an anaphylactic or life-threatening reaction to something that they eat. This is fairly rare for the most obvious of reasons. If every time you eat a peanut, you stop breathing, you are not going to eat very many peanuts. You will either stop or you'll be dead. So, it is pretty much a self-limiting problem, except that children get blind-sided by the presence of the food they weren't aware of. Where food allergy was relatively unheard of 100 years ago, it is becoming more common today, so much that there are mothers who have organized to make sure that their child's environment is completely free of suspect foods like peanuts. Some mothers are aware of the fact that their children are made allergic by milk, but largely, true food allergy is a pretty unusual occurrence, at least in my experience.

➢ SEASONAL ALLERGY AND FOOD REACTIONS

Allergy patients tend not to be very *sick*. Allergy is sort of an "elective illness." Accordingly, they frequently do not come into the doctor's office over holidays. Over the years, my wife, who was an avid golfer, decided that since very few patients came in over the Christmas and New Year holiday, that would be a great time for us to go to Hawaii for the week to play golf, and we started doing that. At that time of year, I have my worst allergies to cedar trees. When we left Austin, I would be terribly sick with allergy, and six hours after we landed in Hawaii, I was full of energy, absolutely bulletproof. I could eat anything, drink anything, run long distances, stay up most of the night, all the while feeling terrific! I was full of energy because there was no cedar pollen in the air in Hawaii. Islands do not have clouds of pollens or molds or they would be barren rocks. Evolution has caused the pollen and mold on islands to be as heavy as a stone, so that the pollen drops to the earth immediately or the winds would carry it right off the islands. The minute we arrived back to Austin, the minute the plane landed, my head began to swell, and I was right back in the bag. I had to start being very careful, *again*, about food. Most of my patients already know that if they travel 100 miles, in *any* direction, their airborne allergy starts to clear up. If their airborne allergy clears up, then they probably don't have to worry about their foods. But when they are in Austin, in the middle of their allergy season, and if they are having symptoms, that is generally when they come to see me. The quickest relief I can provide them will occur within 48 hours of the time they begin to restrict certain foods.

➢ FOODS TO AVOID

The foods that we restrict are the ones to which most allergy patients react. Basically, that includes the following eight food groups:

1. Dairy Products – milk, cheese, yogurt, and ice cream
2. Citrus Fruits and Juices – oranges, grapefruit, lemons and limes
3. Tomatoes and Tomato Products – all tomato products including pizza, pasta, hot sauces, ketchup, and fresh tomatoes
4. Brown Colas – Coca-Cola, Dr. Pepper, Pepsi-Cola, etc.
5. Chocolate – candy bars, chocolate milk and drinks, chocolate in any form
6. Grains – wheat, barley, oats, rice, and corn; chips, bread, cereal, pasta; no grains of any kind.
7. Sugar –candy, sweets, table sugar, fruit juices, soft drinks (*clear* diet soft drinks are okay)
8. Eggs

When they do this, within 48 hours the patients normally notice a dramatic clearing of their symptoms. I can assure the patients this will happen because in 30 years, only five times have patients restricted these foods and told me that they did not feel any better. If I get a patient to restrict these eight food groups for five days, they are going to feel remarkably better because they are stopping some of the hypersensitivity reaction that results from the acid stomach caused by their airborne allergy. I suggest a five-day period for food restriction because it coincides with the school or work week. It also coincides with another strange phenomenon that occurs over the five-day period. When we do not eat a food to which we are allergic, our body continues to make antibodies to it as if we had eaten it and this goes on for *about* five days. It goes something like this: If patients are reacting to milk, then every day their body makes five antibody "cops" to attack the five portions of milk "robbers" they drink. If they stop drinking the milk and they (and their bodies) continue this for five days, we are going to have 25 milk cops waiting for those five gulps of robbers. When they drink the milk after avoiding all dairy for five days, the sky will fall in on them. They will have huge symptoms, more than they have ever had before. It serves no purpose to avoid suspect foods for longer than five days because those antibody responses rapidly go down after the five days. Doctors have occasionally suspected food sensitivity, in particular dairy, or chocolate. The classic test was avoidance for 30 days followed by re-introduction. This rarely resulted in a positive reaction. I think this reflects the rapid slowing of the antibody (cop cells) production after about 5 days.

We have found that probably the *optimal* number is five or six days of avoidance of the "suspect" foods. We get little people (and big people) to restrict the eight food groups starting each Sunday afternoon, and they do not eat any of the foods that I suspect they might be allergic to until Friday night. Friday night, I want them to select the several foods they missed the most; this will typically include their worst food sensitivity, because the foods to which we are allergic are highly addictive. I want the patients to eat whatever they missed the most during the five days of food avoidance. We want to elicit a *huge* reaction to impress upon them the fact that *something* in their usual diet is making them allergic. If they test just one food and have a *little* reaction, they are not going to be very impressed. Thus, I want them to select more than one of the foods they missed the most. This will almost always produce the kind of reaction we are seeking. Now, if they really have a severe reaction, we can reverse it in seconds with our antidotes: buffered vitamin C powder, magnesium (i.e., Epsom salts), Alka-Seltzer Gold, club soda, or baking soda. All these things will reverse a food reaction within seconds of the time that they swallow it. If this patient experiences a dramatic reaction (like a stuffy nose or increased stomach discomfort), maybe he or she is sensitive to one or more of the foods avoided.

I am trying to help the patients see that if they have symptoms, foods might play a role in those symptoms. It is not my job to tell them what NOT to eat; my job is to show them what foods might do. I would like them to experience what food reactions might do so they can make their own choices. My patients learn that if they restrict or avoid foods they are sensitive to during an allergy season, they are going to feel better and better. Their memory will be better. Their mood will be better and their allergy symptoms will be easier to control.

So, when a little kid comes racing home from school, makes a beeline for the refrigerator, and yells out in a loud voice, "Where's my grape juice?" This could be a clue that the child reacts to grape juice. If we see this kind of addictive attraction to a specific food or drink, I suggest Mom try a close substitute. Instead of the favorite grape juice, make sure apple juice is the only thing available, for five days. Then you can try the grape juice again. If people have a sensitivity to something, their symptoms will increase within seconds of the test drink. In kids, the increase in symptoms is often a hyperactive response.

Citrus fruits, juices, and pineapple are terribly reactive because they are already acidic; they already have a low pH. The most common food reaction in my experience is dairy, in particular, cow's milk. We are the only mammals on earth that drink milk after we are weaned. No other mammal does that. We are the only nation in the world that has prominent athletes and actors appearing on magazine pages with a white upper lip . . . "Got milk?" This is the only nation in the world that calls "dairy" (and that includes eggs) a *food group*. We are the laughing stock of the International Scientific Community. Across the world, scientists refer to the food groups as protein, fat, and carbohydrate. In this country, we say the food groups are protein, fat, carbohydrate, and . . . dairy. Dairy? How did this happen? I suppose tobacco would also be a food group if Liggett and Myers had had as powerful a lobby 100 years ago as The American Dairy Association had. Only in this country do doctors insist that children need milk for calcium. We get calcium from almost all of our food. We can even use calcium supplements if needed. However, I think the most *common offender* as a food allergy that I see, especially in kids, is cow's milk. This is such a simple test: five days off the dairy, then try it.

There is no gold standard for food testing. Skin tests are notoriously inaccurate because food does not typically react in a skin reaction like pollen and mold. Blood tests are not accurate and often show allergies to foods the patient can eat without getting any symptoms. Likewise, there are problems with elimination diets to determine hypersensitivity. If we eat anything very long, we will eventually become allergic to it; that means a patient with food allergies might start to itch after two weeks of eating manna from heaven.

Food restrictions and dietary changes are simply a tool we use to help clear up patients. Consider that you are sitting in a boat that will hold you and two rocks afloat. If you add a third rock, you and the boat "sink." There are "too many rocks in your boat." If you have an allergy "attack," like an asthma attack or a severe migraine, it is as though your boat sank. I use this illustration to help patients understand that there is rarely a single cause (a single rock) that explains the attack. It is almost always a combination of things . . . several rocks. I use the example of the Texas cowboy who comes in to me in January and says, "Doctor, I have cedar allergy and I want you to fix it." I tell him that is fine but I would like him to avoid eight groups of food. He says, "You are not paying attention. The only thing that bothers me is cedar and that's all I want to talk about. My stuffy nose has nothing to do with any food." I ask him what he means and he says, "Well, I have chili every morning for breakfast, I have bar-b-que every afternoon for lunch, and I have bourbon and French fries for supper every night of the year. The only time I have trouble is in January." I tell him the Mountain Cedar is like the third rock in his boat. If one of your rocks is your food (let us assume I might be right), a second one is bourbon, and along comes a third rock, Mountain Cedar, and your boat sinks, you say "It is the Cedar." I say, "I can fix this but it is going to take me several days to clear up your stuffy nose using nasal sprays and other medications. On the other hand, I can remove the food rock by tomorrow and that alone will very quickly clear things up and your boat will be afloat again." You can quickly be free of your allergy symptoms if you remove "the last rock" in the boat.

I suggest food restriction for all new patients and any patient with increased symptoms. I suggest beginning the restrictions on Sunday and staying off all the suspected foods on "school nights." So, stay ff the foods from Sunday until Friday. Friday night, pick one or two things you have missed the most. This will probably be something we are quite sensitive to because we tend to *crave* things to which we react. By Friday you will have probably built up quite a craving for something you have been restricting. If you are craving milk and you are sensitive to it, avoiding it five days will set up a bigger than usual reaction. Maybe a very big reaction. The reaction could be anything from a stopped up nose to chest tightness or stomach pain. This increased reaction is referred to as "unmasking the food allergy" by Dr. Marshall Mandell in his book 5-Day Allergy Relief System (HarperCollins, 1988).

I have observed this for the last 30 years that I have been doing this. If I take severe asthmatics and stop feeding them, in 24 hours they will be clear of their asthma symptoms simply by eating no food at all. We used to put everyone on a fast for five days with no food. Well, some people got seriously ill and we realized that was not a good plan. So now, we simply avoid eight groups of food for the five days. My patients are instructed to avoid the eight groups each week from Sunday until Friday night. We do this every week or at least until we're sure of which foods may be causing reactions.

Food restriction is a "tool" we use. It buys us time to get control of airborne allergies. It makes antihistamine more effective. It makes nose spray more effective, and it will make most of us feel better. Generally, the last thing on our minds when we feel bad is food restriction.

➢ FOOD ALLERGIES AND CRAVINGS

Food allergies are usually very precise. We crave what we are allergic to. If you are reacting to chocolate, you probably know exactly what you need to satisfy this craving. I know I react to chocolate. But it's not just "chocolate" . . . it's dark chocolate. Dark, semisweet, Godiva chocolate. I can't resist it. You surround me with white chocolate but I would rather eat Vaseline than the white stuff, or milk chocolate for that matter. But, the Godiva dark . . . hoo boy! I'm a goner. So, I don't let it near me. When we do not feel good, the very thing we are most allergic to makes us feel relief. If a heroin addict wakes up in the morning and he is having a terrible day, he needs heroin; the alcoholic needs a drink; I need dark chocolate, regular Coca-Cola, or strong coffee and I will feel dramatically better. However, I have learned my lesson. If I drink a regular Coke in the morning, I need another one two hours later, and this is an endless situation. So, we need to avoid the things to which we are most allergic. My basic response when I feel bad is simply to stop eating. I can fast for one or two days and feel so much better. That buys me the time to start thinking straight and not buy the yogurt with fruit at the bottom (a personal weakness), but instead to do the other things I know I need to do to control the allergy.

Food sensitivity, while it is terribly common, is usually not really critical in the grand scheme of things, except as a tool for clearing up symptoms. If we are very symptomatic, we think of enzyme reactions as what we call a geometric progression; they go faster and faster and faster. If the tissue in your nose is reacting to airborne things, I can fill your nose with nose spray and it is not going to have any impact; the reaction is too fast. Let's say you are unloading your boat at the lake and it has a long, long cable going down to the lake. All of a sudden, the boat gets out of control and that handle on your winch is flying around just like an airplane propeller. Nothing will stop that action, nothing. That boat is flying down the ramp as fast as it can go. We both know that if we could just stop that action for 1/10 of a second, then a matchstick would keep it from going further. But first, we have to stop the reaction. We do that with the sublingual drops and with food restriction. Food restriction takes a little longer; sublingual drops are instantaneous. If during food restriction or the drops we stop that enzyme reaction (we stop that wild flight of the boat down the ramp), then anything, even a grain of corn in that gear will keep it from going forward. When it is in full flight, you can put a monkey wrench in it and it will fling it out to the side. What we want to do is stop the immediate reaction. The quickest way is the drops and the next best one is the foods (air cleaners are very effective as well); we are going to do all these things to get the patient symptom-free.

Once we get these patients symptom-free, then good sense takes over and they start eating things that they know do not cause a reaction.

If you were standing in line at the cafeteria and they lined up 10 vegetables, I would want you to rank them for the one you like the most to the one you like the least, then select out of the middle four. I want the ones that do not speak to you, positively or negatively. I do not want foods that call out to you to eat them, and I do not want you to eat the ones that you know make you sick. Pick the dull foods. Most people in our society do not respond to foods like I do or like my patients do. Foods to me have a serious drug effect. I know that if I drink red wine or eat a pizza, I will feel like I have been hit in the forehead with a hammer. This does not happen to very many people, but if you are one of them, you really need to find out what foods might be causing your symptoms.

Many people have food addiction, drug addiction, and/or alcohol addiction; this is because these things have a drug effect on them and make them feel better. Few are the people who drink because it makes them feel worse. They drink because it makes them feel *better*. If it makes you feel *a lot* better, then chances are you are going to drink *a lot*. My patients who have allergies are highly adrenalized, and they want to relax at night; they are going to find something that relaxes them. Alcohol relaxes me, pizza relaxes me, chocolate relaxes me, Rocky Road ice cream relaxes me so much it makes me unconscious in a matter of minutes; we all learn the things that work for us. Small children learn this early on; mothers know right away what their kids are allergic to because it is what they demand. If the mother of a child who is sensitive to Coca-Cola, brings home Nehi Cola, there is going to be a huge battle. Mom will be going right back to the store and get the "real" Coke so she won't have to deal with her little "addict." These allergies are highly specific and very addictive. Traditional allergists are quick to point out that these are not "true allergies" and they are not really serious . . . in other words, they don't result in severe or life-threatening anaphylactic reactions. And I agree. However, the kind of allergic reaction to food that I am suggesting is "seasonal." It usually only occurs when your seasonal allergies are bothering you. Then you become more sensitive to food you can eat the rest of the year without problems. So food restriction is simply a tool we use to get better control, to buy us time, while we do the traditional things like desensitization of pollen and mold . . . it is just a tool, but a very *effective* tool.

➢ DIETS AND DIETING

I don't believe in "diets." I prefer to think of lifestyle changes. I have followed every diet known to man including amphetamines (big in the 1960s) and the "Phen-Phen" diet. I even did Overeaters Anonymous with the most serious food fascists you will ever hope to meet. I lost weight . . . every time. And, I gained it back . . . every time. So, I don't care what "diet" you follow, so long as you see it as a way of life. Most people know what type of diet works well for them. When they follow that diet, they lose weight. Then they stop the diet and gain the weight back, often gaining more weight back than they lost. Some of my patients are vegetarians. Some are vegans and some are omnivores, like I am. Use whatever has worked for you in the past. Something you can use in the short term for losing weight, but with slight modification, something you can follow the rest of your life to maintain your best weight . . . from now on.

I recommend reaching and maintaining ideal weight, for all patients, for the rest of their lives. This may seem like dreaming "the impossible dream" . . . but we have to make some efforts to reverse the natural effects of aging and lower hormones, side effects like weight gain, fatigue, and diminished sex drive. Most people know what their ideal weight is, or was. I do not tell patients what they should weigh unless they are really out of touch with their bodies. Men are usually more out of touch with this than women. I tell overweight middle-aged men they need to lose a lot of pounds.

They usually tell me they think their weight is "fine." Even though they weigh 60 or more pounds more than they did in their 20s, it has come on so gradually they have gotten used to it. Being overweight contributes to lots of illnesses and symptoms in addition to the usual fatigue and diminished sex drive.

If you are perplexed about diets, I will present here some remarkably effective ones ranked in order of my preference with some additional detail at the end on the first one. The format for the presentation of these diets follows the same format found in Dr. Wansink's book, Mindless Eating. I have adapted that format with my own thoughts on each diet.

Ideal Protein (www.idealprotein.com)

Description	Advantages	Disadvantages
Theory: Four feedings daily of precisely controlled protein that maximizes fat burn while sparing protein (muscles). Involves: "Meal in an envelope" ease for three meals a day. Very low in fat and carbohydrate. Three-phase diet with rapid weight loss during the first stage tapering to maintenance.	Tastes incredibly good! Quite filling. Very easy to prepare using hot or cold water. Over thirty flavors from oatmeal and chili to chocolate pudding and berry drinks. All contain a precise 21 essential amino acids to keep metabolism revved up and facilitate rapid loss of fat. Does not require exercise.	Requires strict adherence to the diet plan and menus. Moderately expensive. Requires a strict change of lifestyle (no snacks other than salad). If you exercise, you have to adjust the protein intake upward.

Mindless Eating, by Brian Wansink, Ph.D. (www.mindlesseating.com)

Description	Advantages	Disadvantages
Theory: Visual impressions influence our eating habits. This recent (2006) bestseller will make dieting much more effective for you whatever plan you choose to follow. Through very interesting studies, Dr. Wansink demonstrates time after time that we don't realize the diet pitfalls that surround us. When you realize all the psychological triggers that affect eating, you will be able to plan more carefully and lose weight with little effort. You will see how using a smaller plate or glass will cause you to feel full sooner and therefore eat or drink less than you would with the same size portion on a larger plate or in a short, squat glass. This provides some amazingly effective ways to trick your mind into feeling full on less.	Eat less of the same portions by simply reducing the size of the plates and glasses.	You are going to need new dinnerware and some tall, thin glasses.

The Southbeach Diet, by Arthur, M.D. (www.southbeachdiet.com)

Description	Advantages	Disadvantages
Theory: Careful selection of fats and carbohydrate restrictions can result in weight loss. You can improve your cardiovascular health by eating fewer fats and carbohydrates. Diet emphasizes eating the right types of fats and carbohydrates. Three phases from rapid weight loss to maintenance in as little as six weeks. Well-balanced traditional diet designed by a cardiologist. Ordinary food items with few restrictions.	Recipes are provided and easy to prepare. Meals are easy to take with you and can be carried in a brief-case. Regular meals and snacks are requires to ease hunger and maximize weight loss.	Carbohydrates and sugars are severely restricted. Requires strict adherence and lifestyle change.

Weight Watchers Points Diet (www.weightwatchers.com)

Description	Advantages	Disadvantages
Theory: you can eat any food you wish so long as you do not exceed your calculated caloric needs. Eat any food you wish so long as you count the total "points" (calories). Group meetings and support, as well as weekly weight record.	Vegetarians can eat all their usual foods. No excluded foods (including sugar). Can easily be followed at home or eating out.	Requires skill at weighing and measuring. Slow, but steady, weight loss. Requires long-term commitment.

Sugar Busters Diet (www.sugarbustersdiet.com)

Description	Advantages	Disadvantages
Theory: Avoid sugar. Generally, a traditional diet. A balance of fat, protein, and carbohydrate.	Simply modifies your ordinary diet. Teaches you what sugars to avoid (refined ones). Emphasizes healthy lifestyle, including exercise.	Fairly moderate weight loss. No quick fix. Requires an increase in moderate exercise to be successful.

The Zone Diet, by Barry Spears, M.D. (www.zonediet.com)

Description	Advantages	Disadvantages
Theory: Athletes who follow a formula of 40% carbs and 30% fat and protein obtained optimum strength and condition. Suggests weight loss can be achieved by regulating insulin levels with this mix. Weight and measurements of foods are required	Allows a complete mix of food groups. Teaches avoidance of simple sugars. Teaches portion control and ratio balancing. Allows vegetarian diet.	Possibility of weight gain for people over 30. Designed for NCAA athletes. Fairly complicated, requiring some knowledge of nutrition and food values.

Dr. Atkins New Diet Revolution, by Robert Atkins, M.D. (www.atkins.com)

Description	Advantages	Disadvantages
Theory: The fastest way to lose fat is to eat 100% fat. The granddaddy of all low carbohydrate diets. I and many of my patients used this with success for over 20 years. Suggests that if we do not eat any carbs, our bodies will be forced to break down storage fat to get the carbs we have to have each day. Breaking down fat will result in ketone bodies measureable in the urine, a measure of success.	Very rapid weight loss. Many diet choices, all high protein and fat, no carbs. Proven successful for over 30 years. Many products available in stores including complete meals.	Allows large amounts of saturated fat in diet. Unbalanced diet difficult to follow for very long (even I get tired of ribeyes). Serious side effects can include acid stomach, bad breath, nausea, dizziness. Requires lab testing to protect kidneys and liver. Not possible for vegetarians or those who do not have strong stomachs.

The Ideal Protein Diet is my absolute favorite method of "dieting" and the one I use daily. I first heard about this from a research associate, Dr. Michael Ciells, in the fall of 2007. He called me and told me of a remarkably tasty diet using precise formulations of the 21 essential amino acids we need to keep our metabolic rate firing at an optimal level. He told me it was the usual set of pre-packaged meals in foil envelopes with one traditional meal daily, carefully prescribed to be low in fat and low in carbohydrates. It was designed by a Parisian physician, Dr. Tran Tien Chanh. The product was further developed by a famous French chef who had five popular restaurants serving gourmet French food in Quebec, Canada. I consider this the key to the success of the diet in that this stuff tastes wonderful. It is all vegetarian and there are over 30 flavors and meals. Each meal is carefully balanced to provide maximum protein using essential amino acids and minimum fat and carbohydrate. For my evening meal, I can eat four ounces of red meat or six ounces of chicken or fish. I can also have a 12-ounce portion of certain vegetables. During this meal and anytime all day long, you can eat as much salad as you wish. They have a great Web site and you can find sources all over the United States, Canada, and South America.

For background, I read Dr. Tran Tien Chanh's book, The Unbalanced Diet Approach to a Slimmer You. This book is available on the www.idealprotein.com Web site. Dr. Tran (M.D., Ph.D.) focuses on the pancreas' hypersecretion of insulin in response to a carbohydrate load in overweight, usually hyperinsulinemic individuals. He specializes in sports medicine and his doctorate is in nutrition and physiology. This unique diet program is easy and doesn't require a lot of money.

Dr. Chanh lives and practices in Paris, France and originally designed this protocol for Olympic athletes over 20 years ago. He has clinics using his protocol in eight European countries, has a big movement in Canada for the last seven years, and has recently brought the so-called "Ideal Protein Diet" to the United States. His protocol made sense to me, and after refreshing myself on the metabolic effects of insulin and insulin resistance, some of these unexplainable benefits our patients were experiencing began to give up their secrets. The book Protein Power (abbreviated title) by Drs. Michael R. and Mary Dan Eades helped me look at these things from a different perspective. They talk a lot about the balance between insulin and its counterpart glucagon and the notion of "insulin dominance and glucagon dominance."

Apparently, this diet helps maintain the balance. This may be a reason one doesn't gain the weight after achieving our ideal weight. I began the diet Valentine's Day of this year weighing in at 268 pounds. I was okay with that in that I felt good and played a lot of racquetball, did Pilates four times a week, and felt like I was in terrific shape. But, I wanted to weigh less. Over the years, it has been harder and harder to get the weight off and keep it off. So I started the Ideal Protein Diet. Two months later, I was down to 224 pounds. I had lost 44 pounds (mainly fat) and I lost eight inches from my waist. I attribute a lot of this to Pilates and about two hours of aerobic exercise most days of the week; however, I was doing that before the diet and not losing an ounce. Several of the ladies in my office have been doing the diet and everyone has been successful in varying degrees.

The best news is that now, three months later, I have only gained a few pounds back, and I seem to have "re-set" my weight at this new point. I continue to follow the diet to the extent that I eat a packaged meal for breakfast and lunch. However, I can now eat pretty much whatever I want for my evening meal, although I still tend to follow the rule of low fat and low carbohydrates.

Chapter 7

Your Body: An Owner's Manual

We have included in this book a number of things that relate to pain, the relief of suffering, and overall good health. The older we get, the more we have to pay attention to things that really didn't seem important earlier in our lives. Hormone imbalance and allergy are very real, yet very correctable problems. However, we actually bring upon ourselves a number of problems that have absolutely nothing to do with imbalances and allergy conditions and that are very easy to address. All it takes is a little knowledge and a little conviction. Our health is, for the most part and in a very real sense, in our own hands.

We have spent a considerable amount of time talking about reducing stress, changing your diet, and using exercise (the right kinds for the right reasons) to allow your body to appropriately utilize its natural (or replaced) hormones for maximum relief of unwanted pain and other symptoms. These are all very, very important; important enough that we will spend another chapter here re-emphasizing those points. If you get nothing else from reading this book, please learn that much of what ails you might be fixed with no *medical* treatment, and no *surgery* . . . at all. I think you can do it yourself. After all, who wouldn't feel better, *whatever* is wrong with them, if they ate a healthy diet, exercised daily, and said their prayers? What we will attempt to do in this chapter is offer some suggestions that will help you as you make these modifications in your life. Change is not easy; nobody likes change (well, except a baby with a wet diaper), and most of us have a natural resistance to making changes in our lives.

➢ GET UP – SHOW UP – DO IT

When we take Kindergarten or first-grade kids out for the first day of school and the bus rolls up, mothers don't ask, "Honey, would you like to go to school today?" Rare is the child who wants to leave home to go out into a new and unfamiliar world. If Mom were to ask that, most children would say, "No" and make a beeline back into the house. Instead, Mom sets their tiny bottoms on the bus and says, "You can tell me all about it when you get home tonight." That is how we have to approach healthcare. You simply have to suit up, show up, and do it.

First of all, let's start with Rule No. 1: You must *move* to get better. If you cannot move at all, if you cannot walk at a slow pace, if you cannot slowly pedal an exercycle, I cannot help you. Do not make an appointment. I am terribly sorry, but our program will not work for you. You have to be able to move. It helps if you can restrict your foods. It helps if you can pay attention to the things to which you are allergic, but the movement is *critical.* I recommend walking for an hour before bed. If patients will do nothing but the movement, I would say nearly all of them are going to feel 50% better within 30 days. If they do everything else (diet, hormones) but not the movement, they will see nothing near the improvement they would have if they had. Movement is the cornerstone of everything else. The rest builds on the movement. Have I made my point?

I remember so clearly the lady from Boston who came to me with terrible migraines. She could not get out of bed, except one day a week; the rest of the time, she spent in emergency rooms or the doctor's office getting injections of narcotics and lying in a darkened room. I asked her if she was aware of anything that might cause these headaches. She said that red wine always caused the headache. I asked her how often she had red wine and she said . . . "Twice a day." I was surprised to hear her say this. She knew the red wine was at least part of the cause of her headaches, yet she still drank red wine. There are obvious answers to at least some of our problems that we are simply unwilling to consider. This is why I say food sensitivity is so important. If you feel wonderful and full of energy and you are having no allergy symptoms at all, then why would you or anybody care what you ate or drank? On the other hand, if you feel bad, your *first instinct* should be to restrict foods, drink water, and move more. I'll say it again, when you feel bad, *change something.* Most often, your problem is something you are eating or drinking – or you are simply not getting enough physical movement in your daily activities.

We get many patients who contact us on the Internet. I have patients from the United States, Canada, England, Switzerland, and all over South America. One of our clinical instructors, Dorothy Dreux, answers most of their emails, always pointing out our basic requirement before they come. We want them to spend 30 days doing their daily walking at night before they go to bed (the LSD approach); we want them to do the food restriction plan mentioned in Chapter 6; and we want them to keep a daily diary. We also remind them to say their prayers. We find that well over half of them never need to come; they clear up their own symptoms.

➢ CHANGING YOUR LIFESTYLE

We are NOT offering a cure; we are NOT offering a marvelous new medication, unless the drops help, then you may indeed be given a marvelous new medication. We are suggesting a *lifestyle* change. Everybody knows they feel better when they move, but many do not feel like they can move; it hurts or they are too tired. We are saying you *must* move. You are not going to feel any more tired if you move just a little or move really slowly. If you hurt worse, move even more slowly; but you must *move*. Many patients who start moving do not need me, and they figure this out. They generally can handle the rest on their own. All we have to do is start moving. Yes, if you leap up and try and do pole vaults, you are going to get hurt and feel worse; but how about if you got up and just shuffled to the bathroom and sat back down? Let's say you did that every hour and then tomorrow, you did it every 30 minutes, slowly, ever so slowly, so you do not increase the pain. Then gradually (very gradually) you increase the amount of movement and the length of time you continue it. Ultimately (and maybe even immediately), you can and will feel better. You know, what I'm suggesting is indeed counterintuitive – if you're tired, move more. Are you kidding me? How is that possible? Most of the patients I see are trying to move too fast. If you move slowly, you'll gradually regain your strength.

What I am suggesting to the patients and what I have told you in this book is very simple. Most people's symptoms are caused by an imbalance in their hormones. This is particularly true of patients who have been told by their doctors that they can find nothing wrong with them. This is the most common problem I see in my patients. If your doctor tells you there is nothing wrong with you, I would offer you another possibility . . . maybe he is wrong. Mmm. Maybe you have an imbalance caused by low hormones, caused by stress, caused by adrenalin. Maybe that could be corrected by balancing the hormones, addressing the stress and adrenalin, movement, and diet. We want you to restrict the intake of foods that can cause adrenalin to be released. It is generally clear to all of us that cigarettes, coffee, sugar, and chocolate can cause an increase in adrenalin and make us feel worse. (Okay, maybe you feel better . . . but only at first). So, if we go in the other direction and eat a healthy diet of organic foods and drink nothing but water, then we are surely going to feel better.

➢ SOCIAL AND SPIRITUAL DEPENDENCY

Another suggestion concerns the fact that we generally do not do well taking care of ourselves. I am my worst patient. When I am sick, if I get isolated, whatever is bothering me is just going to get worse. I cannot remember what to do for these symptoms. If I can just get to my office and tell the nurses how I feel, they will recognize my allergy symptoms at once and remind me of the correct diet and movement to deal with it. We can help others, but there is something about helping ourselves that is more difficult. Most likely, you are not going to be able to solve your own problem; but if you can talk to a friend with similar problems, if you can talk to your naturopath, your homeopath, your internal medicine doctor, your minister, or whomever it might be, somebody will be able to give you some advice and you are going to recognize it. Most health advice for these symptoms is just what your mother told you; it is what your grandmother told you. So, it may be that your best "doctor" is your Mom, your fitness coach, your racquetball partner, or your walking buddy. Walk with a friend. You are more likely to show up. When I have a racquetball game scheduled, even if I do not feel like it, I am going to show up because the other person expects me to be there. If you have a walking partner with whom you are doing your exercise, you may not feel like walking, but you will go anyway to support them and they will support you. I think it is very important to get involved in some kind of physical activity, to restrict your diet, and to find some doctor with whom you can talk about lifestyle changes. If you cannot talk to your doctor, talk to your dentist, talk to your minister, your rabbi, your priest, but do not try to do this on your own.

In India, if an elephant goes insane, they chain it between two sane elephants. After a year, the elephant is just fine. So, we tell people they have to get back into life. You have to resume a healthy lifestyle; you have to *act* as if you are not tired. I want every one of my patients to *move*. I want them to restrict their foods. I want them to have a social life, a spiritual life, and an intimate or sexual life. We want them to *act* as if they feel better because I think that in many cases just acting as if you feel better actually causes you to feel better. If I wake up every morning and tell myself my life is a tragedy and I just cannot bear to go to work, then my life will be a tragedy and I will not be able to bear going to work. If, on the other hand, I get up every morning and I say "Thank you, God, for giving me this day, and I will try to do the best I can with it," my life is ging to be a wonderful event that is filled with good things. We get what we expect to get. There really is something to the *power of positive thinking*! I try to help patients understand that they should expect a lot out of their lives, regardless of their condition. I don't care if you're a cancer patient, or somebody with broken bones, or leprosy . . . if you walk more, have a social life, have a spiritual life, you're going to feel better. If you isolate yourself and don't move, you are not going to improve your health. And that is what I run into time after time with my patients. Consequently, we tell all patients, "When you come, we will try and instill in you the confidence to try and make changes by getting rid of your symptoms right away; but if you can't come, try these things anyway." If I get rid of your symptoms, then I'm going to convince you that you *aren't really sick*. Maybe you can get moving, maybe your fatigue is caused by inactivity, maybe your pain is caused by stress which can be relieved by low level activity, by a better attitude, and by a more complete social life. So, when you come, we are going to tell you that your doctor was right, you aren't really sick. The patients come and they are hoping that I will discover some really rare disease that their doctor missed and I'll give them a pill and they'll be well. We say, "You know, it doesn't work like that, and I can tell you right now – you *aren't sick*! Isn't that marvelous news? So, let's get on with your life, let's start moving, let's eat correctly, let's have a more joyous life!" We get just what we expect to get. *It really is in your head, and that's the good news.* Yes, it is all in your head just like your doctor has told you. What seemed negative, however, is really positive. If it's all in your head, you can fix it, and very quickly. But we have to change what you are doing. We want to get rid of the negativity. People are often steeped in negativity because their doctor has given them large doses of it. Worse yet, he gives them drugs that are ineffective, at best, and quite often make them even worse. I've had some patients who are on 20-24 medications, prescribed by six different doctors who haven't talked to each other! Some of them are repeating or doubling diuretics, and the patient is wondering why they are dizzy, have blurred vision, and muscle cramps. The third doctor does not even ask which medicines they are on or didn't even look at their chart. Pain medicine on top of pain medicine; antidepressants stacked on top of antidepressants – just a tragedy. And you know what? When you take two to three chemicals, your body breaks them down, and chemical fragments may recombine to make new chemicals with totally unique results. We get these overdosed patients who don't have a clue which way is up. The first thing we do is start cutting out medications. Doctors medicate the symptoms, not the causes.

Lastly, we need to talk about an element that is of extreme importance and that goes hand-in-hand with all of the lifestyle modifications we have recommended. This final piece to the puzzle is spirituality. Some call it "religion." Whatever you want to call it, it is an important part of healing the mind and the body of what ails it. Most of my patients either go to church or believe in God. I say, "Great! Why would we want to overlook that important tool?" Over the past 40 years, numerous scientific studies have supported the notion that spirituality, regardless of its kind or nature, improves health and actually increases longevity of life. It cannot be refuted that incorporating spirituality into one's life helps one live a happier and healthier life. Maybe it is the serenity that the believer has in the power of prayer. Regardless of what it is about spirituality that produces the effect, the effect is very real. We have discussed the importance of *balance* in this book. Granted, for the most part, we were discussing our hormones; but we also have alluded to a balance in other parts of our lives: stress, diet, and exercise. To these we now add spirituality.

Chapter 8

Your Options

These are my observations – I have been there and I know what the patient is going through. I think patients are much more impressed and confident if the doctor treating their problems is empathetic. I don't think a doctor has to have had cancer to treat cancer . . . but it helps. I don't think that is a requirement, but that certainly makes me more empathetic and willing to listen to their complaints more than a doctor who has not experienced similar problems. We are never going to get totally over all the symptoms that plague us. There will always be problems and symptoms we will have to deal with. However, as long as we drink carefully, eat carefully, and do an hour of low-level exercise, every day, we can get by in this world with a relative degree of comfort. If I can make the serious pain go away or get down to a bearable level, if I can help you breathe comfortably, you might give me a month to correct the underlying causes of the problems, to reduce your stress, to change your diet, to address your allergies, in particular your pregesterone-medieated inflammation. And that is what I am counting on. I have a window of opportunity when a new patient comes in. They say, "Well, I've gone this far, I might as well try it." It is a wonderful experience to be able to see people who have been suffering for years, who have given up hope on traditional medicine, and who have decided they will live with this pain (or worse) the rest of their lives, take just one important step and try what we offer. Indeed, I am most fortunate; I know every day that I live and work, I make someone's life more tolerable at the least, and at best, I give them back the lives they knew prior to their affliction. Life has so much to offer that is good, and we do not have to settle for living it in pain and suffering.

➢ TRADITIONAL MEDICAL DOCTORS

Where can you find a doctor who agrees with me? Well, this is not going to be easy. First of all, you need a doctor that will talk to you . . . and listen . . . to you. It might be a relative; it might be your family doctor. For women, it might be their OB/GYN. You will know right away if you can talk to your doctor or not. When many doctors are made uncomfortable by things they do not know or that are different from their own training, they become defensive. They might become angry, they might even be threatening to the patient; but once in awhile, you run into a doctor who is empathetic with you and, as a result, you feel comfortable talking with them. There are many doctors who are empathetic with these principles, but they do not understand them. Once you find a doctor who will talk these things over with you, you need to arrange a time when they are not busy and you can visit with them about your symptoms and about some of the things about which you might have read on our Web site. Practically everything that I have told you in this book is available on my Web site. We offer these instructions to any doctor who wants the information and it is available at no charge. It is laid right out on the Web site at www.robyinstitute.com. We tell them how to do it, how to approach it, how to make antidotes, how to use the sublingual drops. The entire thing is available to any doctor who wants to do it. I am perfectly happy to talk to any doctor who wants to talk to me. On several occasions, I have sent the drops to doctors and clinics when they expressed interest, usually at the urging of a patient of theirs who read about our treatments on the Internet.

About once a month, a doctor will call me. I will tell you that there is an almost tangible feeling of disbelief. They are usually skeptical, probably because these methods and results seem just "too good to be true." However, some doctors are willing to experiment, particularly since we are not talking about using drugs at all. If the doctor is open-minded and if he is willing to pay attention to these things, then you may find somebody who is willing to try and help you in your quest for better health. Keep in mind, we are not talking about diseases and we are not talking about drugs; we are talking about some real common sense things like exercise and diet, possibly sublingual drops, and hormone balancing. There are many doctors out there who agree with the concept of bioidentical hormones; you will know immediately when you call a doctor's office and ask them about these things. Chances are good that somebody is going to hang up on you if they do not agree. If they do agree, they will be quite pleased to make that clear to you. There are definitely doctors who are willing to try new things. The vast majority are not interested.

Most doctors are so busy doing what they do, and doing such a good job for so many patients, that they have no time for this sort of thing. What they do works very well for most of the patients that they see, so why should they take an hour dealing with you, when they can see six office visit patients in the same time doing for them what they do very effectively. They are very busy, they are very well rewarded, and it is very gratifying for them to treat people with "real" diseases with effective remedies. If you start out with the recognition, however, according to the lab test, that you do not have a disease, then there is really not much they have to say to you. There is also, on the other hand, the possibility that you have been diagnosed with a real disease like Behcet's Syndrome, or multiple sclerosis, or polymyositis, or pulmonary fibrosis . . . and the diagnosis is incorrect.

What if you have been diagnosed with one of these terrible disorders and you are told there are no clear causes and there is no known treatment? It is pretty clear that autoimmunity plays a role in these disorders and that inflammatory reactions are taking place. What if one of the major causes of the reactions is progesterone-mediated inflammation? What if the symptoms could be dramatically reduced in a matter of seconds by blocking this progesterone-mediated inflammation? With sublingual hormone drops? There are no side effects to this type of test. It works or it doesn't. In my offices we get a dramatic reduction in the twelve symptom categories we set out at the end of Chapter 1. Three out of four patients see this dramatic improvement seconds after we administer the drops. That is a higher success rate than we would see in the general population because my patients already know they have a hormone problem.

However, suppose all patients who went to the pulmonologists' offices with shortness of breath were screened with sublingual drops. Screened as they were signing in. If the shortness of breath went completely away, they wouldn't even need to see the doctor, much less get a battery of tests and x-rays and lung scans. Maybe one in 20 or one in 10 would be completely cleared up. Wouldn't that be a good thing? For the patient it would. But, the doctor might see it differently. That would mean a significant reduction in the number of patients he treats, particularly the chronic problems that are not resolved by drugs like prednisone and albuterol. These are the very patients we are most successful at treating.

I have delivered this information to national meetings of the Pan American Allergy Society in 2004 and 2005. I delivered these findings at a poster presentation at the American College of Allergy, Asthma and Immunology (2004). I know of three physicians who are using these methods in this country. Not one physician stopped to view my presentation at the American College meeting. Not one. These methods have been adopted widely in Brazil, where my paper "Progesterone as a Bronchodilator" was published. Dr. Shilpa Shah uses this method in Mumbai, India. Why not here?

I have given up taking this to doctors. Instead, I aim the message at the patients. The sufferers of interstitial cystitis have a national associate and many active support groups and blogs. So do the pulmonary fibrosis patients. I will publicize this on the Internet appealing directly to the patients. I point out that I offer this, at no charge, if their doctor will try it on them. If they cannot find a doctor who will try it, I invite them to come to one of our clinics. If the tests do not reduce their symptoms, there is no charge at all. If they elect to be treated, we offer a money back guarantee at any time. These tests are

SAFE

EFFECTIVE

INEXPENSIVE

➢ THE MEDICAL "COP-OUT"

When I was in medical school, we were told that some patients had a serious "emotional overlay" and that they needed psychiatric help; that is the doctor's favorite "cop-out." If they cannot figure out what is wrong with you, if you do not respond to treatment, then there is something wrong with your emotions and your head needs "shrinking," or "You need a psychiatrist." At this point, your doctor will often suggest an antidepressant. After all, you certainly seem depressed. Well, of course you are depressed: you do not feel good and no one is really doing anything that is helping you. You might even be told that you have a really serious problem, which is invariably fatal, and there is nothing that can be done for you. That would certainly be a good reason to be depressed. But what about the depression of one who is told, "There is nothing wrong with you. It is all in your head." Is there a psychiatric reason for the depression? Did somebody die? Did somebody get divorced? Or have you simply drifted into depression and hopelessness due to feeling terrible, being overweight, having lost your sex drive, having lost the affection of your partner, having screaming kids, and having a job that is terribly stressful? These things are depressing but they may not require an antidepressant. They require a different approach. Traditional medicine isn't cutting it and traditional physicians think you are crazy. What we offer is a different approach . . . a completely different approach. We want to find out the causes of the problems.

➢ WHAT WE DO

If we can treat the causes of your symptoms, if we block the symptoms, then you feel better, fast. We can determine the causes by seeing which symptoms are reduced by which sublingual tests. We'll then look at your hormone levels to see what might be the problem there. Most of our patients have at least one hormone that is out of balance and as we have said, one out of balance can cause a host of problems even with the other hormones. We then will look at other factors that might be negatively affecting your health. We examine your allergies, your stress levels, your diet, and your exercise levels. We will treat you with whatever is necessary to address your problems and put you on the road to health and well-being. Our patients leave the office feeling better than when they entered; a few leave absolutely pain free, breathing much better, or with no symptoms at all. We block symptoms with sublingual drops. This is a test and an early part of the treatment. It is a test in that we can tell what hormone problem you might have by determining which sublingual hormones most effectively block your symptoms. Patients are sent home with those same drops so they can manage their symptoms while we address the underlying causes of the progesterone-mediated inflammation. We put your hormones back into balance, back to where they are supposed to be, back to where they were before you had problems.

New patients are tested and treated on their first visit. This visit takes approximately three hours and includes both testing and instruction. Most patients return home and will not need to see us for approximately one year, as we will test annually to see if there are continuing problems of any sort. Forty percent of our patients need no follow–up treatment after their first visit.

In ten years, I predict that these screening tests will be as common as blood pressure readings and weight and temperature measurements. I think that in a few years we will need a lot fewer physicians for a lot fewer sick patients.

The Roby Institute
4407 Bee Caves Road
Suite 122
Austin, TX 78746
(512) 338–4336
(800) 842–6349
http://www.robyinstitute.com

Author's Note

More than likely, you will need to read this book (or certainly parts of it) more than once. You have encountered here a number of new and very different ideas concerning your health and what to do about it. You will likely forget much of what you have read here that will need reinforcement. Researchers tell us that on the average we forget 70-90% of what we read. Fortunately, you now have this resource that you can use as often as you need to and that will allow you to take charge of your health and manage it effectively the rest of your life. The model on the opposite page will provide you with an at-a-glance version of the Roby Method.

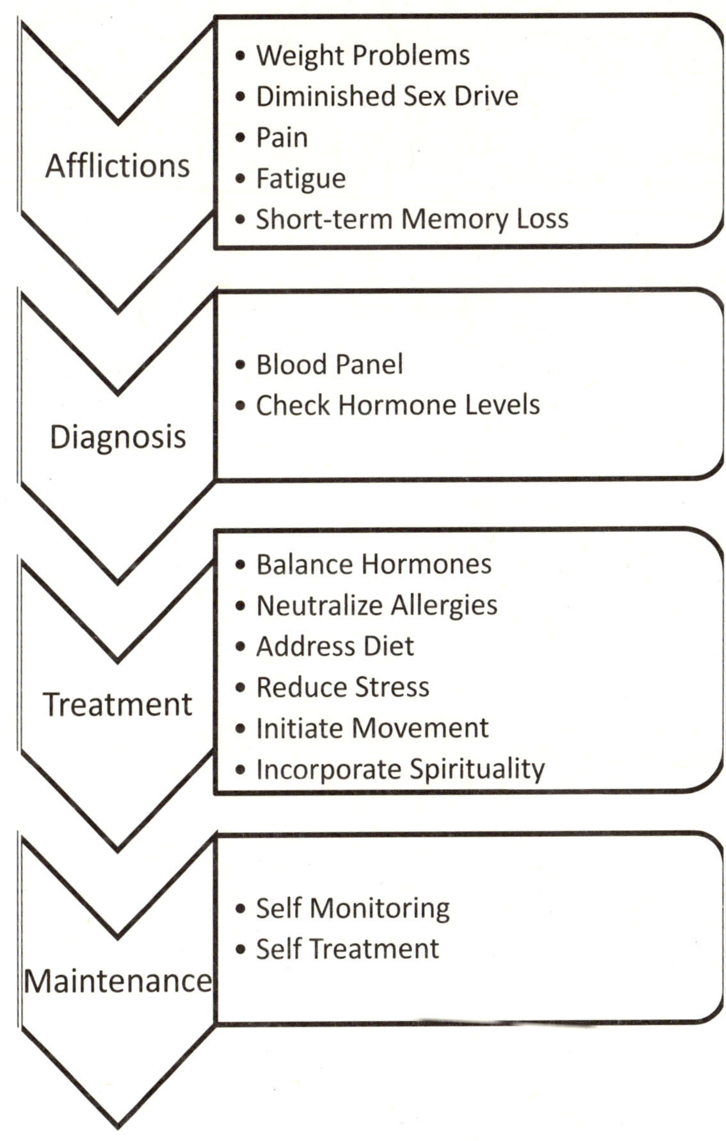
Afflictions
• Weight Problems
• Diminished Sex Drive
• Pain
• Fatigue
• Short-term Memory Loss
Diagnosis
• Blood Panel
• Check Hormone Levels
Treatment
• Balance Hormones
• Neutralize Allergies
• Address Diet
• Reduce Stress
• Initiate Movement
• Incorporate Spirituality
Maintenance
• Self Monitoring
• Self Treatment

Index

C

D

E

F

G

H

I

J

L

M

N

O

P

R

S

T

U

V

W

X

Authors/Scientists/Doctors Cited

Books/Web Sites Cited

Organizations Cited